Your Happy Healthy Pet™

Parakeet

2nd Edition

Julie Rach Mancini

Howell Book House™

Library of Congress Cataloging-in-Publication Data:

Mancini, Julie R. (Julie Rach)
 Parakeet / Julie Rach Mancini.— 2nd ed.
  p. cm. — (Your happy healthy pet)
 ISBN-13: 978-0-7645-9919-4 (cloth)
 ISBN-10: 0-7645-9919-4
 1. Budgerigar. I. Title. II. Series.
 SF473.B8M2795 2005
 636.6'865—dc22
                           2005020234

Printed in the United States of America

10 9 8 7 6 5 4 3 2 1

2nd Edition

Edited by Beth Adelman
Photo research by Marcella Durand
Book design by Melissa Auciello-Brogan
Cover design by Michael J. Freeland
Book production by Wiley Publishing, Inc. Composition Services

About the Author

Birds have been an important part of **Julie Rach Mancini**'s life ever since her father built a window shelf to feed pigeons as mealtime entertainment for her when she was a toddler. Her parents got her first bird, a parakeet named Charlie, when she was six, and she kept a special African grey parrot named Sindbad for more than ten years. Professionally, her interest in birds began to combine with her love of writing when the editors of *Pet Health News* asked her to write about bird health in 1988. She assisted in the preparation of the first issue of *Birds USA*, a successful annual publication aimed at the first-time pet bird owner, and became managing editor, then editor, of *Bird Talk* in 1992. Julie has been a freelance writer since 1997, with pets as her primary focus.

About Howell Book House

Since 1961, Howell Book House has been America's premier publisher of pet books. We're dedicated to companion animals and the people who love them, and our books reflect that commitment. Our stable of authors—training experts, veterinarians, breeders, and other authorities—is second to none. And we've won more Maxwell Awards from the Dog Writers Association of America than any other publisher.

As we head toward the half-century mark, we're more committed than ever to providing new and innovative books, along with the classics our readers have grown to love. This year, we're launching several exciting new initiatives, including redesigning the Howell Book House logo and revamping our biggest pet series, Your Happy Healthy Pet™, with bold new covers and updated content. From bringing home a new puppy to competing in advanced equestrian events, Howell has the titles that keep animal lovers coming back again and again.

Contents

Part I: The World of the Parakeet   **9**

Chapter 1: What Is a Parakeet?   **11**
Parakeet Basics   12
Why Choose a Bird?   12
Parakeets and Children   15

Chapter 2: The Parakeet's History   **17**
Birdkeeping Through the Ages   17
The Parakeet's Background   18
Why Is the Parakeet So Popular?   20

Chapter 3: Choosing Your Parakeet   **22**
Where Will You Get Your Parakeet?   22
Choosing the Right Parakeet   24
Signs of Good Health   *25*
Bringing Your Parakeet Home   27

Part II: Caring for Your Parakeet   **29**

Chapter 4: Home Sweet Home   **30**
Choosing a Cage   30
Setting up the Cage   *36*
Location, Location   37
More to Buy   38
Safety Around the House   42

Chapter 5: Everyday Care   **46**
Be Alert to Health Indicators   47
Cleaning the Cage   *48*
Seasonal Needs   49
Traveling with Your Bird   49

Chapter 6: Feeding Your Parakeet   **52**
A Healthy Diet   52
Don't Feed These to Your Bird!   55
Sharing People Food   55
The Pelleted Diet Option   56
Introducing New Foods   *57*
Grit   58
Supplements   58
What About Water?   59

Chapter 7: Grooming Your Parakeet   60
  Preening   60
  Bathing   61
  Nail Trimming   62
  Wing Trimming   62
  Molting   63
  Wing Trimming Step by Step   64
  If Your Bird Escapes   66
  Are Mite Protectors Necessary?   68

Chapter 8: Keeping Your Parakeet Healthy   69
  Avian Anatomy   69
  Parakeet Senses   75
  Visiting the Veterinarian   76
  Signs of Illness   78
  Medicating Your Parakeet   80
  Alternative Health Treatments   81
  Parakeet Health Concerns   82
  Parakeet First Aid   87
  Your Parakeet's First-Aid Kit   91
  Can You Catch Avian Flu from Your Bird?   94
  Caring for Older Birds   95
  When Your Parakeet Dies   96

Part III: Enjoying Your Parakeet   99
Chapter 9: Parakeet Behavior   100
  Common Parakeet Behaviors   100
  Stress   105

Chapter 10: Having Fun with Your Parakeet   107
  Taming Your Parakeet   107
  Toilet Training   111
  Naughty Parakeets   111
  Will My Parakeet Talk?   112
  Tricks to Teach Your Parakeet   116

Appendix: Learning More About Your Parakeet   120
  Books   120
  Magazines   121
  Online Resources   121
  Bird Clubs   121
  Pet Loss Resources   122

Index   123

Shopping List

You'll need to do some shopping before you bring your new bird home. Below is a basic list of the supplies you must have on hand. For more detailed information on how to select each item, consult chapter 4. For specific guidance on what grooming tools you'll need, review chapter 7.

☐ Cage

☐ Open food and water bowls (at least two sets of each for easier dish changing and cage cleaning)

☐ Perches of varying diameters and materials

☐ Sturdy scrub brush to clean the perches

☐ Food (a good-quality fresh seed mixture or a formulated diet, such as pellets or crumbles, plus fresh foods)

☐ Millet spray (most parakeets love this treat!)

☐ Powdered vitamin and mineral supplement to sprinkle on your pet's fresh foods

☐ A variety of safe, fun toys

☐ Cage cover (an old sheet or towel that is free of holes and ravels will serve nicely)

☐ Playgym (to allow your parakeet time out of her cage and a place to exercise)

There are likely to be a few other items that you're dying to pick up before bringing your bird home. Use the following blanks to note any additional items you'll be shopping for.

☐ _____

☐ _____

☐ _____

☐ _____

☐ _____

☐ _____

☐ _____

☐ _____

☐ _____

☐ _____

Pet Sitter's Guide

We can be reached at (___)_____-_____ Cell phone (___)_____-_____

We will return on _____ (date) at _____ (approximate time)

Bird's Name _____

Species, age, sex _____

Important Names and Numbers

Veterinarian _____ Phone (___)_____-_____

Address _____

Emergency vet _____ Phone (___)_____-_____

Address _____

Poison Control _____ (or call vet first)

Other individual to contact in case of emergency _____

_____

Care Instructions

Use these lines to let the sitter know what to feed, how much, and when; when to give treats; and when and how to exercise your bird.

Morning _____

_____

Afternoon _____

_____

Evening _____

_____

Medications needed (dosage and schedule) _____

_____

Any special medical conditions _____

_____

Grooming instructions _____

_____

My bird's favorite playtime activities, quirks, and other tips _____

_____

_____

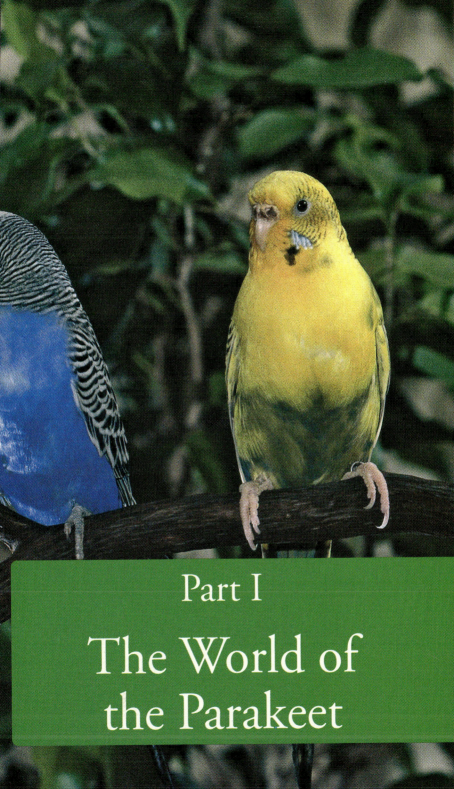

Part I
The World of the Parakeet

The Parakeet

Nare

Cere

Beak

Crown

Breast

Nape

Foot

Mantle

Nail

Covert Feathers

Rump

Flight Feathers

Tail Feathers

Chapter 1

What Is a Parakeet?

Welcome to the wonderful world of parakeets! For many people, parakeets are their introduction to the fascinating hobby of birdkeeping. Some people move on to larger parrots after they become comfortable with caring for a parakeet, while others specialize in raising parakeets in pairs or small flocks.

The parakeet I had as a child, Charlie, was my first pet, and what I learned while keeping him led me to also adopt dogs, cats, a guinea pig, and the occasional tank of fish while I was growing up. After I graduated college and began working at the company that publishes *Bird Talk* magazine, an opportunity presented itself for me to adopt an African grey parrot named Sindbad who had special needs. The birdkeeping skills I learned while caring for Charlie helped me greatly in caring for Sindbad, and I appreciated each bird for the special individual he or she was.

This book will help you set up a healthy and interesting home for your parakeet. It will guide you in selecting a healthy bird and offer advice on feeding and grooming your pet. It will explain the importance of regular veterinary care and look at some common parakeet health problems. Finally, it will look at normal parakeet behaviors and offer some advice about how to teach your parakeet to do tricks.

If you feel the urge to become a bird owner and you've bought this book instead, you're on the right road. If you bought this book along with your parakeet, this is also a good first step. If you've picked up this book after having your bird a few weeks or months, congratulations! You're on the road to responsible bird ownership.

Parakeets are the most popular companion bird in the United States, and one of the most popular pet birds in the world. Those of you who are new to pet birds are probably wondering just what a parakeet is and what all the fuss is about. Let's meet this little treasure.

Parakeet Basics

A parakeet is a long-tailed small parrot from Australia. He measures about seven inches long. In the wilds of Australia, this little bird is green. But breeders began developing different colors in the 1870s in Europe, and the parakeet is now available in a rainbow of colors, including yellow, blue, white, violet, and olive green.

Parakeets have been kept as pets for more than 160 years, since John Gould brought the first live birds to Britain from Australia. Some forty-five million parakeets are kept as pets around the world today, entertaining their owners with their active antics and their ability to learn tricks and to talk. Through the years, parakeets have performed in bird circuses, helped educate schoolchildren about basic pet care in classrooms, and brightened the lives of seniors and others in pet therapy programs.

Why Choose a Bird?

Before you decide to bring a parakeet into your life, you'll need to ask yourself a few questions. Do you like animals? Do you have time to care for one properly? Can you have pets where you live? Can you live with a little mess in your home (seed hulls, feathers, and discarded food)? Can you tolerate, and appreciate, a little noise (the amount made by one exuberant parakeet) as part of your daily routine?

If you answered yes to all these questions, you're a good candidate for bird ownership. Your next question might be, "Why do I want a bird?" Here are some of the answers.

Birds are relatively quiet pets. Unless you have a particularly vocal macaw or cockatoo, most birds aren't likely to annoy the neighbors the way a barking dog can. In the case of parakeets, you'd need quite a large flock to disturb your neighbors because parakeets have quiet, chirpy little voices. In many rental leases, birds may not

Parakeets have chirpy little voices and won't make a racket.

The Parakeet at a Glance

Native land: Australia

Also known as: budgerigar, budgie, shell parrot, warbling grass parakeet, zebra parrot

Length: seven inches from the top of the head to the tip of the tail

Weight: thirty grams (1.06 ounces)

Life span: up to 18 years

Colors: Parakeets come in a wide variety of colors, including bright green (their native color), olive green, dark green, sky blue, cobalt, white, yellow, and violet. Other color varieties (known as mutations) include cinnamon, lutino (bright yellow feathers, clear red eyes, pale yellow beaks, and pale pink legs), white wing, lace wing (red eyes and lacy, light brown markings on the wings), yellow wing, opaline (less-prominent head striping, a V-shaped area on the back that is free of markings, and darker wing feathers), and spangle (wing feathers that are lighter in the center and darker on the edges).

even be considered pets because they are kept in a cage much of the time. This means you may be able to keep them without having to surrender a sizable security deposit to your landlord.

If you're a bird owner who rents an apartment or a house, you may be able to get your current landlord to write a letter of reference for your birds that you can use to show future landlords, explaining how responsible you are as a bird owner and how well-behaved your bird has been.

Birds' small size makes them good pets for today's smaller living spaces. More of us are living in apartments, mobile or manufactured homes, or condominiums, which makes it awkward and inconvenient to keep a large pet who needs a yard and lots of regular exercise. Birds just seem to fit better in apartments, condos, mobile homes, and other smaller living spaces.

Birds interact well with their owners. Although a bird isn't as blindly loyal as the average dog, he is far more interactive than a fish, a hamster, or even a guinea pig. As an added bonus, many birds can learn to whistle or talk, which is unique among pets and which many bird owners find amusing and entertaining.

> **Parrot Traits**
>
> The parakeet is a species of parrot, and all parrots have certain traits in common:
>
> Four toes on each foot—two pointing backward and two pointing forward
>
> The upper beak overhangs the lower beak
>
> Broad head and short neck

Birds are long-lived pets. A cockatoo named King Tut greeted visitors at the San Diego Zoo for seventy years, and *Bird Talk* magazine reported on a 106-year-old Amazon parrot in Alaska. Many bird owners I know have made provisions for their larger parrots in their wills. Smaller birds can live long lives, too; the *Guinness Book of Records* reports an almost 30-year-old parakeet in Great Britain.

Birds require consistent, but not constant, attention. This can be a plus for today's busy single people and families. While birds can't be ignored all day, they are content to entertain themselves for part of the day while their owners are busy elsewhere.

The needs and companionship of a bird provide a reason to get up in the morning. The value of this cannot be overestimated for older bird owners and single people who are on their own. Birds provide all the benefits of the human-animal bond, including lower blood pressure and reduced levels of stress.

Birds are smart, social animals, and they may surprise you with how affectionate they can be.

The Bottom Line

Keeping a companion bird is a big responsibility. Here are some things you need to think about as you become a parakeet owner.

- The cost of the bird himself
- The cost of his cage and accessories
- The cost of bird food (seeds, formulated diet, and fresh foods)
- The cost of toys
- The cost of veterinary care
- The amount of time you can devote to your bird each day
- How busy your life is already
- Who will care for the bird when you go on vacation or are away on business
- How many other pets you already own
- The size of your home

Finally, birds are intelligent pets. Whoever coined the phrase "birdbrain" didn't appreciate how smart some birds are. On intelligence tests, some larger parrots have scored at levels comparable to chimpanzees, dolphins, and preschool-age children.

Parakeets and Children

If you plan to purchase a parakeet as a child's pet, please keep the following in mind. Children in the primary grades need some help from their parents or from older siblings to care for their new pet. Children in the intermediate grades should be ready for the responsibility of bird ownership with parental supervision. Or the bird can just be a family pet, with each family member being responsible for some aspect of the bird's care. Even the youngest family members can help out by selecting healthy foods for the bird on a trip to the market or picking out a safe, colorful toy at the bird store.

Parents need to remind children of the following when they're around birds:

- Approach the cage quietly. Birds don't like to be surprised.
- Talk softly to the bird. Don't scream or yell at him.
- Don't shake or hit the cage.
- Don't poke at the bird or his cage with your fingers, sticks, pencils, or any other items.
- If you're allowed to take the bird out of his cage, handle him gently.
- Don't take the bird outside. In unfamiliar surroundings, birds can become confused and fly away from their owners. Most are never recovered.
- Respect the bird's need for quiet time.

I'd like to remind adults to please not give a live pet as a holiday present. Birthdays, Christmas, Hanukkah, Easter, and other holidays are exciting but stressful times for both people and animals. A pet coming into a new home is under enough stress just by joining his new family; don't add to his stress by bringing him home for a holiday. Instead, give your child pet-care accessories for the actual celebration and a gift certificate that will allow the child to select his or her pet (with parental supervision, of course) after the excitement of the special day has died down.

Homing Parakeets

The noted British aviculturist the Duke of Bedford raised a large flock of parakeets on his country estates in Great Britain in the 1950s. The birds became known in avicultural circles for their homing abilities—talents more often associated with racing pigeons. The duke would let the birds loose to fly freely each morning, and they would return to their roosts in his aviaries by nightfall. He developed his flocks by selecting birds who showed even temperaments and weren't prone to flying off wildly when set free.

Chapter 2

The Parakeet's History

Parakeets have been kept in captivity for more than 160 years—the longest of any companion bird species—and are considered by many birdkeepers to be truly domesticated, thanks to their long association with people. But birdkeeping goes back much longer than that.

Birdkeeping Through the Ages

The ancient Egyptians are credited with being the first to keep birds, most notably pigeons. Queen Hatsheput (1504 B.C.–1482 B.C.) was the first monarch to create a royal zoo, which included exotic birds. In the fifth century B.C., a court physician and naturalist in the Persian Empire wrote about talking birds that were described to him by Indian merchants.

From Egypt, birdkeeping spread to Greece and Rome. Alexander the Great receives credit from some historians for first describing and taming the Alexandrine parakeet, and the Greeks are credited with popularizing parrot-keeping outside of the birds' native lands of Africa and Asia. Well-to-do Romans built extensive garden aviaries, and also kept mockingbirds in the entryways of their homes as feathered doorbells to announce visitors. The Romans are thought to have been the first bird dealers, bringing different types of birds to the British Isles and the European continent.

Birdkeeping has fascinated people for thousands of years.

Until the Renaissance, birdkeeping was a hobby that only the wealthy could pursue. After canaries were introduced into Europe by Portuguese sailors in the 1500s, though, birdkeeping began to take off as a hobby, although it was still confined largely to upper-class fanciers.

In the 1600s, the Dutch began breeding varieties of canaries for show. These birds were exported to Britain, and birdkeeping began to be more accessible. At about the same time, in the British penal colony of Australia, a forger named Thomas Watling first described the parakeet's ability to mimic human speech. The bird he described was able to greet Watling's employer by saying, "How do you do, Dr. White?"

In the Victorian era, bird sellers in the British Isles offered goldfinches and larks to ship captains en route to the West Indies. These common European birds would then be traded in the islands for species found there.

The Parakeet's Background

Now that we've looked at the history of birdkeeping, let's look at the background of your chosen bird, the parakeet. Some of you may know parakeets by their more official name—budgerigar. Whatever you call them, these small, perky parrots are among the most popular pet birds in the world.

True Australians

Parakeets come from Australia, where they live in large communal flocks. (These large flocks make parakeets naturally sociable birds. If you keep a single pet bird, make sure you fulfill her need for companionship by spending time with her every day.) Many wild parakeets are found in central Australia, which is a harsh, arid land. To cope with these extreme conditions, parakeets have adapted to surviving on minimal food and water requirements. (Notice that I say surviving and not thriving. Parakeets kept in captivity need more than seeds and water to thrive.)

The parakeet's British name, budgerigar, is said to come from an Aboriginal phrase that means "good to eat," although I can't imagine eating such personable little birds. The species' scientific name, *Melopsittacus undulatus*, means "song parrot with wavy lines," which refers to the birds' melodic voices and the wavy bars across their backs and wings. These wavy lines help wild parakeets camouflage themselves in the Australian grasslands so they are less visible to predators.

The Parakeet Arrives in Europe

The British naturalist John Gould is credited with bringing the parakeet to the attention of the pet-loving public. In 1838, Gould and his wife, Elizabeth, traveled from London to Australia to study the continent's native wildlife for a series of books Gould was writing. Although he considered parakeets to have rather dull personalities, Gould brought a pair back to Britain.

Parakeets soon became popular pets with upper-class Europeans, and hundreds of thousands of them were sent on weeklong sea voyages from Australia to Britain, Belgium, and Holland. Although many birds died in transit, those who survived proved to be surprisingly easy to breed in captivity (Gould's brother-in-law, Charles Coxen, bred the first pair in Britain in the 1840s), and they were soon being bred across Europe by zoological gardens and aristocratic birdkeepers. One of the first pair bred by Coxen was sold by a British bird dealer for twenty-seven pounds sterling—the equivalent of several hundred dollars today.

The Antwerp Zoo in Belgium was one of the first places where parakeets were put on display. Parakeet breeding began in earnest in Antwerp in the 1850s, and it soon

No Imported Budgies

Although many parrot species were imported into North America from their native lands until the late 1980s, parakeets have not been exported from Australia since 1894. All parakeets sold as pets in America are domestically bred and raised, which makes them better pets than wild-caught animals.

spread across Europe. France imported one hundred thousand pairs of birds, and breeding farms were set up in France and Belgium by the end of the nineteenth century.

Despite all this breeding, parakeets were still being exported by the thousands from Australia to Europe, South Africa, South America, and the United States. Australia finally banned the export of parakeets in 1894—a ban that is still in force.

Parakeets in America

Although they have been kept as pets in America for years, parakeets began their current reign of popularity in the United States in the 1950s. Today, about 17.3 million pet birds are kept in American homes, and 45 percent of them are parakeets, according to statistics from the American Pet Product Manufacturers Association. They are the most widely kept pet parrot in the world, with some five million pet and show birds in Great Britain alone.

Why Is the Parakeet So Popular?

Some of the reasons bird lovers are attracted to parakeets include their manageable size, their gentleness, their nondestructiveness, the ease with which they can be handled and tamed, their sociable nature, and their ability to talk—although the last shouldn't be the sole reason for choosing a parakeet or any other pet bird.

English and American Parakeets

In your search for the perfect pet parakeet, you may have noticed that there are two types of parakeets: English and American. The differences between the two birds are small but noticeable. English budgerigars (or budgies) tend to be larger, more majestic, and less active, while American parakeets are smaller, livelier, and more likely to be found in most pet stores. American breeders tend to raise more American than English parakeets, because the demand for the American variety is greater.

The English budgerigar (right) is larger than the American parakeet, but they're both the same bird.

A parakeet's size makes her an easily handled pet for bird lovers, young or old. This small size comes with a quiet, pleasant voice and a manageable beak. Since the loud voice and the potential for painful bites that come with larger parrots deter some would-be bird owners, the parakeet offers a welcome alternative.

Because parakeets have been kept as pets for so many years, some people consider them one of the few domesticated pet birds. They seem to enjoy people and being part of an active family. They also seem to want to please their owners by learning tricks or learning to talk, although I can't guarantee that your parakeet will be a trickster or a talker. Ultimately, people choose a parakeet as a pet because they want to share their homes with a bird and appreciate her for the unique being that she is.

Chapter 3

Choosing Your Parakeet

Now that you know a little more about the history of birdkeeping and about the parakeet, you'll need to know how to select the healthy, happy parakeet who is the right pet for you. You'll need to think about whether you want a single bird or a pair, and whether a male or a female is right for you.

Where Will You Get Your Parakeet?

There are several ways you can get a parakeet, including classified newspaper advertisements, bird shows and marts, and pet stores. Let's look at the pros and cons of each in detail.

Classified Ads

Classified ads are usually placed by private parties who want to sell pet birds. If the advertiser offers young birds, it is likely to be a private breeder who wants to place a few birds in good homes.

Baby parakeets have a series of stripes that cover their heads and necks (the stripes remain on the back of the birds' necks following the first molt). Young birds have small, slightly elongated spots on their face masks, while adults have large, round spots. Youngsters have large, dark eyes that give them particularly endearing looks, while adult birds have well-developed white irises. Baby parakeets may also have dark or slightly black beaks.

Some breeders may also offer older birds for sale from time to time. These are most likely breeder birds who are too old to produce chicks but who are still good candidates for pet homes.

Bird Shows and Marts

Shows and marts offer bird breeders and bird buyers an opportunity to get together to share a love for birds. Bird shows can provide prospective bird owners with the chance to see many different types of birds all in one place (usually far more than many pet shops keep at a time), which can help you narrow your choices if you're undecided about which species to keep. At a bird mart, various species of birds and a wide variety of birdkeeping supplies are offered for sale, so you can go and shop to your heart's content.

Pet Stores

Pet stores can be a good place to buy a parakeet, but you must do some checking first. You'll need to visit the store and make sure it's clean and well kept.

Make sure the birds in the pet store look healthy, content, and active.

Walk around a bit. Are the floors clean? Do the cages look and smell as if they're cleaned regularly? Do the animals in the cages appear alert, well fed, and healthy? Do the cages appear crowded or do the animals inside have some room to move around?

Did someone greet you when you walked into the store? Is the store staff friendly? Remember that you will be visiting a pet store every week or two to buy food, toys, and other items for your parakeet, so choose a store with friendly, helpful people behind the counter.

Find out what the staff does to keep their birds healthy. Do they ask you to wash your hands with a mild disinfectant before handling their birds or between birds? If they do, don't balk at the request. This is for the health of the birds and it indicates that the store is concerned about keeping its livestock healthy. Buying a healthy bird is much easier and more enjoyable than purchasing a pet with health problems, so look for a caring store and follow the rules.

If something about the store, staff, or birds doesn't feel quite right, take your business elsewhere. If the store and its birds meet with your approval, then it's time to get down to the all-important task of selecting your parakeet.

Choosing the Right Parakeet

Look at the parakeets that are available. If possible, sit down and watch them for a while. Don't rush this important step. Do some seem bolder than the others? Consider those first, because you want a curious, active, robust pet, rather than a shy animal who hides in a corner. Are other parakeets sitting off by themselves, seeming to sleep while their cagemates play? Reject any birds who seem too quiet or too sleepy, because these can be signs of illness.

Remember that healthy birds spend their time doing three main things—eating, playing, and sleeping—in about equal amounts of time. If you notice that a bird seems to want only to sleep, for instance, reject that bird in favor of another whose routine seems more balanced.

You may think saving a small, picked-upon parakeet from his cagemates seems like the right thing to do, but please resist this urge. You want a strong, healthy, spirited bird, rather than the "runt of the litter." Although it sounds hard-hearted, automatically reject any birds who are being bullied, are timid, hide in a corner, or shy away from you. It will save you some heartache later.

If possible, let your parakeet choose you. Many pet stores display their parakeets in colony situations on playgyms, or a breeder may bring out a clutch of babies for you to look at. If one bird waddles right up to you and wants to play, or if one comes over to check you out and just seems to want to come home with you, that's the bird for you!

Male or Female?

You may be asking, "Should I get a male or a female parakeet?" Although males may be slightly better talkers, I'd encourage you to get a young, healthy bird of either sex and enjoy your companion for his or her full pet potential. If you have your heart set on an older bird, males generally have blue ceres (the bare patch of skin over the parakeet's beak), while females' ceres are brownish. Don't try this sexing test on a young bird, because cere color develops as a bird matures.

The male, in front, has a blue cere, while the female, in back, has a brown cere.

One or Two?

Another question you may have (especially if you have a busy schedule) is, "Should I get one bird or two?" Single parakeets generally make more affectionate pets, because you and your family become the bird's substitute "flock." But a pair of parakeets can be pretty entertaining as they encourage each other into all sorts of avian mischief. And if you are away from home all day every day, your two birds will keep each other company.

Signs of Good Health

Here are some of the signs that a parakeet is healthy. Keep them in mind when you are selecting your pet.

- Bright eyes
- A clean cere (the area above the bird's beak that covers his nares, or nostrils)
- Clean legs and vent
- Smooth feathers
- Upright posture
- A full-chested appearance
- Bird is actively moving around the cage
- Good appetite

Leg bands help identify a particular breeder's stock and the individual identity of your bird.

One small drawback of owning two pet parakeets is that they may have a tendency to chase each other around the cage, playfully tugging on one another's tail feathers. Sometimes these feathers come out, leaving you with two considerably shorter parakeets until the next set of tail feathers grows in. If you have a pair of birds who suddenly become tailless, check the cage bottom for the feathers and watch your birds to see if they do, indeed, chase and pester each other. If so, you have nothing to worry about. If not, please alert your avian veterinarian to the problem and ask for further guidance.

Two birds are also less likely to learn to talk, because they can chatter to each other in parakeet rather than learning the language of their substitute "flock."

If you do not bring both birds home at the same time, there is a possibility of territorial behavior on the part of the original bird. This territorial behavior can include bullying the newcomer and keeping him away from food and water dishes to the point that the new bird cannot eat or drink.

To avoid this problem, house the birds in separate cages and supervise all their interactions. Let the birds out together on a neutral playgym and watch how they act with one another. If they seem to get along, you can move their cages closer together so they can become accustomed to being close. Some birds will adjust to having other birds share their cages, while others prefer to remain alone in their cages with other birds nearby.

By the same token, don't try to put a new parakeet into the cage of a bird you already own, and don't house parakeets with other small birds, such as finches, canaries, cockatiels, or lovebirds. Parakeets may bully finches and canaries, keeping them away from food and water bowls, while cockatiels and lovebirds may bully parakeets. To keep peace in your avian family, make sure every bird has his own cage, food, and water bowls. Some parakeets will get along with other birds during supervised time on a playgym, while others do not work and play well with others and enjoy being the only pets out on the gym.

Bringing Your Parakeet Home

Although you will probably want to start playing with your new parakeet the minute you bring him home, please resist this temptation. Your pet will need some time to adjust to his new environment, so be patient. Instead, spend the time talking quietly to your new pet, and use his name frequently while you're talking. Move slowly around your parakeet for the first few days to avoid startling him.

You will be able to tell when your new pet has settled into his routine. By observation, you will soon recognize your parakeet's routine and know what is normal. You may also notice that your bird fluffs or shakes his feathers to greet you, or that he chirps a greeting when you uncover his cage in the morning. If your parakeet learns to talk, he may eventually greet you with a cheery "hello" or "good morning" as you uncover his cage.

Quarantine

If you have other birds in your home, you will want to quarantine your parakeet for at least thirty days to ensure he doesn't have any diseases that your other birds could catch. To do this, keep your new parakeet as far away from your other birds as possible, preferably in a separate room. Feed your newly arrived parakeet after you feed your other birds, and be sure to wash your hands thoroughly before and after handling or playing with your new pet. Quarantine is usually just a precautionary measure, but you can't be too safe when your pets' health is involved!

Soon enough, your bird will fluff his feathers to greet you and may even call out "hello."

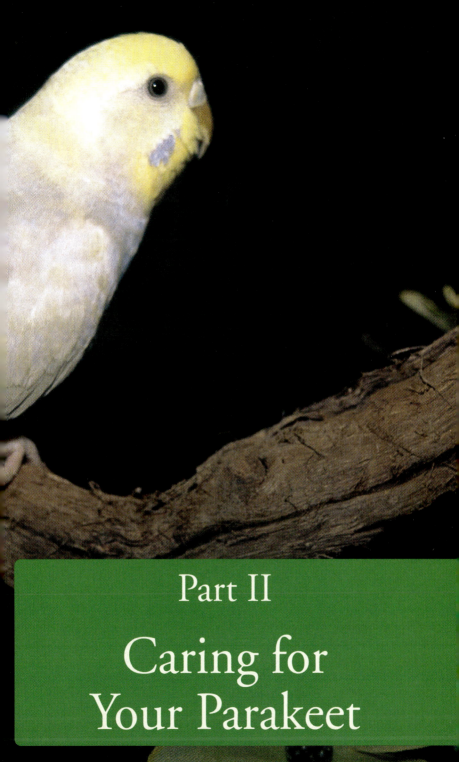

Part II

Caring for Your Parakeet

Chapter 4

Home Sweet Home

Before you bring your feath-
ered friend home, you have a lot of shopping to do. Selecting
your parakeet's cage will be one of the most important decisions you make
for her. You must also decide where she will live in your house or apartment.
Don't wait until you bring your bird home to think this through. You'll want
your new pet to settle in comfortably right away, rather than adding to her stress
by relocating her several times before you settle on the right spot for the cage.

Choosing a Cage

Although we didn't do too many things right for my childhood parakeet,
Charlie, we did select a good home for him. Charlie's cage was large, it had both
horizontal and vertical bars for his climbing enjoyment, his food and water
dishes slid in and out through holes in the side of the cage (which meant they
were easy to get to and made his cage simple to service), it had three or four
perches placed at different heights in the cage, and it had a bedsheet for a cover
at night.

Some of the cages you'll look at while making your selection are designed to
sit on tabletops, while others have built-in or attached stands. Consider which
will work best in your home. If yours is an active house with other pets and children in it, a tabletop cage may be better than a cage with a stand that could be
knocked over. If you live alone in a small apartment, a cage and stand might be
in order. If you do choose a cage with a stand, be sure the stand is steady and fits
well with the cage.

Cage Considerations

Your parakeet will spend much of her time in her cage, so make this environment as stimulating, safe, and comfortable as possible. Keep the following things in mind when choosing a cage for your parakeet.

- Make sure the cage is big enough. The dimensions of the cage (height, width, and depth) should add up to at least sixty inches for a single bird.
- An acrylic cage may be easier to clean up. Wood or bamboo cages will be quickly destroyed by an eager parakeet's beak.
- Make sure the cage door opens easily and stays securely open and closed. Avoid guillotine-style doors.
- The cage tray should be a regular shape and easy to slide in and out. There should be a grille below the cage floor so you can change the substrate without worrying about the bird escaping.

Size Matters

When choosing your parakeet's cage, remember that it must be large enough to house your bird, her food and water bowls, perches, and toys. One way to ensure the cage you choose is large enough is to measure the length, width, and height. When added together, these measurements should total at least sixty inches. That's the minimum for a cage large enough for one parakeet and her accessories. A common size for parakeet cages is eighteen inches wide, eighteen inches high, and twenty-four inches long, which adds up to sixty. This is the smallest cage to consider if you own a single pet bird. If you have more than one bird, or if your bird is an upwardly mobile creature with lots of belongings (toys, food dishes, a bathtub perhaps), a larger cage is in order.

Simply put, buy the largest cage you can afford, because you don't want your pet to feel cramped. Remember, too, that parakeets are like little airplanes, flying horizontally, rather than little helicopters that hover up and down. For this reason, long rectangular cages that offer horizontal space for short flights are preferred to high, narrow cages that don't provide much flying room.

When it comes to cages, the bigger the better.

Acrylic or Wire?

Birdcages are traditionally made of metal wire, but you may see acrylic cages in magazine advertisements or at your local pet store. These cages are better at containing seed hulls, loose feathers, and other debris your bird creates, which may make birdkeeping easier and more enjoyable for you. Although it sounds like a sales pitch, I know from experience that acrylic cages clean up easily by wiping inside and out with a damp towel and regularly changing the tray that slides under the cage itself.

If you choose an acrylic cage for your pet, make sure it has numerous ventilation holes drilled in its walls to allow for adequate air circulation. Be particularly careful about not leaving your parakeet in direct sunlight if you house her in an acrylic cage, because these cages can get warm rather quickly and your bird could become overheated. (Parakeets in wire cages shouldn't be left in direct sunlight either, as they can overheat, too.)

If you go with an acrylic cage, you'll have to include a couple of ladders between the perches to give your pet climbing opportunities she won't be able to take advantage of on the smooth sides of an acrylic cage.

If you find wooden or bamboo cages during your shopping excursions, reject them immediately. A busy parakeet beak will make short work of a wooden or bamboo cage, and you'll be left with the problem of finding a new home for your pet! These cages are designed for finches and other songbirds, who are less likely than a parakeet to chew on their homes.

If you choose a wire cage, examine it carefully before making your final selection. Make sure the finish is not chipped, bubbling, or peeling, because a curious parakeet may find that spot and continue removing the finish. This can cause a cage to look old and worn before its time, and some cages may start to rust without their protective finish. And if your parakeet ingests any of the finish, she could become ill.

Reject any cages that have sharp interior wires or wide spaces between the bars. (Recommended bar spacing for parakeets is between three-eighths and seven-sixteenths of an inch.) Your parakeet could become caught between bars that are even slightly wider than recommended, or she could escape through widely spaced bars.

As for the arrangement of the bars, be aware that some birds may injure themselves on the ornate scrollwork that decorates some cages. And make sure the cage you choose has some horizontal bars in it so your parakeet will be able to climb the cage walls if she wants to exercise.

Your parakeets will enjoy climbing on their wire cage. Make sure the bars are evenly spaced and are close enough together that your bird cannot get caught between them.

Cage Door Options

Once you've checked the bar spacing and the overall cage quality, your next concern should be the cage door. Does it open easily for you, yet remain secure enough to keep your bird in her cage when you close the door? Is it wide enough for you to get your hand in and out of the cage comfortably—with the bird perched on your finger? Will your bird's food bowl or a bowl of bath water fit through it easily?

Does the door open up, down, or to the side? Some bird owners like their pets to have a play porch on a door that opens out and down, drawbridge style, while others are happy with doors that open to the side. Watch out for guillotine-style doors that slide up and over the cage entrance, because some parakeets have suffered broken legs when the door dropped on them unexpectedly.

Cage Tray Considerations

Next, look at the tray in the bottom of the cage. Does it slide in and out of the cage easily? Remember that you will be changing the paper in this tray at least once a day for the rest of your bird's life (about fifteen years, with good care).

Is the tray an odd shape or size? Will you have to cut paper into unusual shapes to fit in it, or will paper towels, newspapers, or clean sheets of used computer paper fit easily into the tray? The easier the tray is to remove and reline, the more likely you will be to change the lining every day. Can the cage tray be replaced if it becomes damaged and unusable? Ask the pet supply store staff or the cage manufacturer's customer service department before making your purchase.

As long as we're on the subject of cage trays, let's talk about what goes in them—the substrate. I recommend clean black-and-white newspapers, paper towels, or clean sheets of used computer printer paper. Sand, ground corncobs, or walnut shells may be sold by your pet supply store, but I don't recommend these as cage flooring materials because they tend to make owners lazy in their cage-cleaning habits. These materials tend to hide feces and discarded food quite well. This can cause a bird owner to forget to change the cage tray on the principle that if it doesn't look dirty, it must not be dirty. This line of thinking can leave time for a thriving, robust colony of bacteria to set itself up in the bottom of your bird's cage, which can lead to a sick bird. Newsprint and other paper products don't hide the dirt; in fact, they seem to draw attention to it, which leads conscientious bird owners to keep their pets' homes scrupulously clean.

On a related note, you may see sandpaper (a.k.a. "gravel paper") sold in some pet supply stores as a cage tray liner. This product is supposed to provide a parakeet with an opportunity to ingest grit, which is purported to help aid digestion by providing coarse grinding material that will help break up food in the bird's gizzard. The problem is that experts are unable to agree on just how much grit a pet bird needs. Many British avicultural books advocate offering a parakeet regular supplements of grit, while American parakeet fanciers are less generous with their offerings because some parakeets have overeaten grit. This causes impacted crop, a serious condition that requires immediate veterinary attention. Additionally, if a bird stands on rough sandpaper when she's on the cage floor, she could become prone to infections and other foot problems caused by the rough surface of the paper. For your parakeet's health, please don't use these gravel-coated papers.

The cage tray should be easy to slide out for daily cleaning. Newspaper makes an excellent cage tray liner.

Cage Floor

Check the floor of the cage you've chosen. Does it have a grille that will keep your bird out of the debris that falls to the bottom of the cage, such as feces, seed hulls, molted feathers, and discarded food? To ensure your pet's long-term good health, it's best to have a grille between your curious pet and the remains of her day in the cage tray. Also, it's easier to keep your parakeet in her cage while you're cleaning the cage tray if there's a grille between the cage and the tray.

The Cage Cover

Be sure you have something to cover your parakeet's cage with when it's time to put her to sleep each night. The act of covering the cage seems to calm many pet birds and convince them that it's really time to go to bed, even though they may hear the sounds of an active family evening in the background.

You can buy a cage cover or you can use an old sheet, blanket, or towel that is clean and free of holes. Be aware that some birds like to chew on their cage cover through the cage bars. If your bird does this, replace the cover when it becomes too holey to do its job effectively.

Setting up the Cage

Make sure you have the cage all set up and ready before you bring your bird home, to help ease the transition for your pet. Here's how to set up your parakeet's cage.

- **Select the right location.** Your parakeet will be more comfortable if her cage is set up in a part of the house that you and your family use regularly, such as a family room. Your parakeet's cage should be out of the main traffic flow of the room, but still part of the room so you can include your bird in normal activities, such as watching TV. (Don't put your bird's cage near the kitchen or bathroom, because cooking and chemical fumes from these rooms can harm your parakeet.)

- **Set the cage up with a solid wall behind it.** Your parakeet will feel more secure if she has a solid wall behind her cage because nothing can sneak up on her from behind.

- **Stagger the perches within the cage.** Don't place all the perches at the same height in the cage because your parakeet will be happier if she can perch at different heights at different times of the day.

- **Arrange the perches correctly.** Don't place perches directly over food or water bowls because pet birds eliminate regularly during the day, and you don't want your pet's food or water contaminated by her droppings.

- **Add some toys.** Your parakeet will need toys in her cage to help entertain her during the day. You should rotate the toys regularly to ensure your bird doesn't become bored with the same toys. You'll also have to replace those that your pet destroys during playtime. Don't overfill the cage with toys because your bird still needs room to move around. She needs to climb around in the cage and maybe even take short flights from end to end for exercise. She also needs to be able to get to the food and water bowls without interference from her toys.

- **Provide a cage cover.** Your parakeet will benefit from having her cage covered when she goes to sleep at night. Covering the cage will help your bird settle down at bedtime, which helps her establish a good daily routine.

Location, Location

Now that you've picked the perfect cage for your pet, where will you put it? Your parakeet will be happiest when she can feel like she's part of the family, so the living room, family room, or dining room may be among the best places for your bird. If your parakeet is a child's pet, she may do well living in her young owner's room. (Parents should still check to make sure she's being fed and watered regularly and that her cage is clean.)

Whatever room you choose, keep the cage out of direct sunlight and place it up against a solid wall so that your parakeet doesn't become stressed by feeling that her home is exposed on all sides.

Avoid keeping your parakeet in the bathroom or kitchen, though, because sudden temperature fluctuations or fumes from cleaning products used in those rooms could harm your pet. Another spot to avoid is a busy hall or entryway, because the activity level in these spots (and the drafts when doors open) may be too much for your pet.

Noise Company

It's important to keep a radio or television on for your parakeet if you leave her home alone for long periods of time. Although parakeets have been kept as pets for about 160 years, they may still instinctively revert to their wild roots at times. In the grasslands of Australia (as in all wild places), silence usually means there's a predator in the area, which can raise a bird's stress level. Because you don't want a stressed-out pet, please leave a radio or television on at a low volume for your parakeet if you will be away, so that she will have some background noise and some variety in her daily routine. Some parakeets may even learn the words to commercial jingles they hear on the radio or TV!

This bird's well-furnished cage is kept where her family gathers.

More to Buy

Along with the perfect size cage in the ideal location in your home, your parakeet will need a few cage accessories. These include food and water dishes, perches, and toys.

Food and Water Dishes

When selecting dishes for your parakeet, be sure to pick up several sets so that mealtime cleanups are quick and easy. Dishes should be washed in hot, soapy water and thoroughly rinsed every day. Seeds and formulated diets should only go in dry dishes, to prevent the growth of mold, so two sets of dishes will make things a lot easier. Bacteria will survive more easily in plastic dishes, so consider stainless steel or ceramic.

Choose only uncovered dishes for your pet's food and water because parakeets are often reluctant to stick their heads into hooded feeders to eat. Some have even starved to death rather than eat from a covered dish.

Perches

Birds spend almost all of their lives standing, so keeping their feet healthy is important. Also, avian foot problems, such as bumblefoot and pressure sores on the soles of the feet, are much easier to prevent than they are to treat after they've become a problem.

When choosing perches for your parakeet's cage, try to buy perches of at least two different diameters and materials so your bird's feet won't get tired of standing on the same size perch made of the same material day after day. Think of how tired your feet would feel if you stood on a piece of wood in your bare feet all day, then imagine how it would feel to stand on that piece of wood barefoot every day for ten or fifteen years. Sounds pretty uncomfortable, doesn't it? That's basically what your bird has to look forward to if you don't vary her perching choices.

The recommended diameter for parakeet perches is half an inch, so try to buy one perch that size and one slightly larger (five-eighths of an inch, for example) to give your pet a chance to stretch her foot muscles.

> **TIP**
>
> **Check the Dishes**
>
> Your bird should have clean water at all times, and this may mean refilling the water dish several times a day. Be sure to check your bird's seed dish daily, as well, to make sure she has seeds, rather than just empty seed hulls, in the dish. Refill the dish when necessary.

When you walk down the bird-care aisle at your local pet supply store, you'll probably notice perches in a variety of materials. Along with the traditional wooden dowels are manzanita branches, PVC tubes, rope perches, and concrete grooming perches. Each has its advantages. And since you will be providing your bird with several perches, you can choose a different material for each one.

Manzanita branches are natural, and so offer birds varied diameters on the same perch, along with chewing possibilities. PVC is pretty indestructible. (Make sure any PVC perches you offer your bird have been scuffed slightly with sandpaper to improve traction.) Rope perches also offer varied diameters and a softer perching surface than wood or plastic. Concrete provides a slightly abrasive surface that birds can use to groom their beaks without severely damaging the skin on their feet in the process. Some bird owners have reported that their pets have suffered foot abrasions with these perches, however, so watch your parakeet carefully for signs of sore feet (signs may include an inability to perch or climb, favoring a foot, or raw, sore skin on the feet) if you choose to use a concrete perch. If your bird shows signs of lameness, remove the concrete perch immediately and arrange for your avian veterinarian to examine your bird.

When placing perches in your parakeet's cage, vary the heights so your bird has different levels to perch at in her cage. Don't place any perches over food or water dishes, because birds will contaminate food or water by eliminating in it.

Birds stand on their feet all their lives, and appreciate a variety of perches in different widths and textures. These birds are on manzanita perches.

No Sandpaper, Please

To help your bird avoid foot problems, do not use sandpaper covers on her perches. These abrasive sleeves, touted as nail trimming devices, really do little to trim a parrot's nails because birds don't usually drag their nails along their perches. What the sandpaper perch covers are good at doing, though, is abrading the surface of your parakeet's feet, which can leave her vulnerable to infections and can make movement painful.

Finally, place one perch higher than the rest for a nighttime sleeping roost. Parakeets and other parrots like to sleep on the highest point they can find to perch, so please provide this security for your pet.

Because perches can sometimes double as chew toys, don't be alarmed if your parakeet suddenly seems to become a feathered termite. She may need more chew toys in her cage, or she may just like destroying perches. In either case, be prepared to make many trips to your pet supply store for replacement toys and perches, and be glad that you have a healthy, well-adjusted parakeet who likes to play.

Choosing the Right Toys

Parakeets need toys to occupy their minds, bodies, and beaks. Accept that your bird will chew on any toy you buy, and that you will eventually have to replace it. When selecting toys for your parakeet, keep a few safety tips in mind.

Size

Is the toy the right size for your bird? Large toys can be intimidating to small birds, which makes the birds less likely to play with them. On the other end of the spectrum, larger birds can easily destroy toys designed for smaller birds, and they can sometimes injure themselves severely in the process. Select toys for your parakeet that are labeled as being for parakeets, finches, or canaries to ensure that they are the appropriate size for your pet.

Safety

Is the toy safe? Good choices include sturdy wooden toys (either undyed or painted with bird-safe vegetable dye or food coloring) strung on closed-link chains or vegetable-tanned leather thongs, and rope toys. If you buy rope toys for your parakeet, make sure her nails are trimmed regularly to prevent them from snagging in the rope, and discard the toy when it becomes frayed to prevent accidents.

Unsafe items to watch out for are brittle plastic toys that can easily be shattered into fragments by a parakeet's busy beak, lead-weighted toys that can be cracked open to expose the dangerous lead to curious birds, loose link chains that can catch toenails or beaks, ring toys that are too small to climb through safely, and jingle-type bells that can trap toes, tongues, and beaks.

> **TIP**
>
> **New Toy**
>
> When you're putting toys in your parakeet's cage for the first time, you might want to leave the toy next to the cage for a few days before actually putting it in the cage. Some birds accept new items in their cages almost immediately, but others need a few days to size up a new toy, dish, or perch before sharing cage space with it.

Social Concerns

Mirrors are found on many parakeet toys, and most birds are fascinated with and enamored of that handsome bird in the reflection. Some birds become so infatuated with "the other bird" that they seem to lose interest in their owners, so you might want to wait until your parakeet is settled in her surroundings and comfortable with you before adding a mirrored toy to her cage.

Homemade Toys

Some entertaining toys can be made at home. Give your parakeet an empty paper towel roll or toilet paper tube (from unscented paper only, please), string some Cheerios on a thong of vegetable-tanned leather, or offer your bird a dish of uncooked pasta pieces to destroy.

Your parakeet needs a place to play outside her cage. A playgym comes with a tray underneath to keep the surroundings clean.

The Playgym

Although your parakeet will spend quite a bit of time in her cage, she will also need time out of her cage to exercise and enjoy a change of scenery. A playgym is just what your parakeet needs to keep her physically and mentally active.

If you visit a large pet supply store or bird specialty store, or look through the pages of any pet bird hobbyist magazine, you will see a variety of playgyms on display. You can choose a complicated gym with a series of ladders, swings, perches, and toys, or you can get a simple T-stand that has a place for food and water bowls and an eyescrew or two from which you can hang toys. If you're really handy with tools, you can even build a gym to your parakeet's size and playing specifications.

As with the cage, the location of your parakeet's playgym will be a consideration. Place the gym in a secure location in your home that is safe from other curious pets, ceiling fans, open windows, and other household hazards. It should be in a spot frequented by your family, so your bird will have company and supervision while she plays.

Safety Around the House

One of the reasons you chose a parakeet as a pet is because she's such a curious, active little bird. This curiosity and activity can lead your pet into all sorts of mischief around your home, some of which can hurt her.

This doesn't mean you shouldn't let your pet out of her cage. On the contrary, all parrots need time out of their cages to maintain physical and mental health. The key to keeping your pet safe and healthy is to watch over her and play with her when she's out of her cage. Both of you will come to enjoy these playtimes greatly.

Household Hazards

Hazard	Risk to Your Parakeet
Unscreened windows and doors	Escape
Mirrors	Collision and injury
Exposed electrical cords	Electrocution if chewed on
Toxic houseplants	Poisoning
Ashtrays	Burns from lit cigarettes; poisoning from ingesting cigarette butts
Venetian blind cords	Hanging

Hazard	Risk to Your Parakeet
Sliding glass doors	Escape if they're open; collision and injury if they're closed
Ceiling fans	Injury
Open washing machines, dryers, refrigerators, freezers, ovens, dishwashers	Death when bird flies into appliance, is trapped and forgotten, and dies when appliance is activated
Open toilet bowls	Drowning
Uncovered fish tanks	Drowning
Leaded stained glass items or inlaid jewelry	Poisoning
Uncovered cooking pots on the stove	Drowning, scalding, poisoning, burns
Crayons and permanent markers	Poisoning
Pesticides, rodent killers, snail bait	Poisoning
Lit stove burners	Burns
Candles	Burns
Open trash cans	Injury by flying into and possibly being tossed out with the trash

Parrot-proofing your home is akin to baby-proofing it. If you consider that the average macaw or cockatoo is intellectually and emotionally a perpetual 2-year-old, you'll have some idea of the responsibility parrot owners take on when they adopt their pets. Although your parakeet is smaller than a cockatoo or a macaw, she is no less curious than her larger cousins and no less precious to you than those larger birds are to their owners, so be aware of the potential dangers in your home.

The dangers don't stop with the furniture and accessories. A plethora of fumes can overpower your pet, too. Try to keep your pet away from anything that has a strong chemical odor, and be sure to apply makeup and hair-care products far away from your parakeet.

To help protect your pet from harmful chemical fumes from cleaning products, consider using "green" alternatives, such as baking soda and vinegar to clear clogged drains, baking soda instead of scouring powder, lemon juice and mineral oil to polish furniture, and white vinegar and water as a window cleaner. Not only will you help your parakeet stay healthy, you'll make the environment healthier, too!

Home remodeling and improvement projects can also cause harm to your pet parakeet. Fumes from paint or formaldehyde, which can be found in carpet backing, paneling, and particleboard, can cause pets and people to become ill. If you are having work done on your home, consider boarding your parakeet at your avian veterinarian's office or at the home of a bird-loving friend or relative until the project is complete and the house is aired out fully. You can consider the house safe for your pet when you cannot smell any trace of any of the products used in the remodeling.

Another potentially hazardous situation arises when you have your home chemically treated for insects. Ask your exterminator for information about the types of chemicals that will be used in your home and inquire if pet-safe formulas are available.

Other pets can be harmful to your parakeet's health, too. A curious cat could claw or bite your pet, a dog could step on her accidentally or bite her, or another, larger bird could break her leg or rip off her upper mandible with his beak. If your parakeet tangles with another pet in your home, contact your avian veterinarian immediately because emergency treatment (for bacterial infection from a puncture wound or shock from being stepped on or suffering a broken bone) may be required to save your parakeet's life.

Owners and other people can unintentionally be a parakeet's worst enemy. At *Bird Talk*, we frequently heard from distraught owners who accidentally rolled over on their pets while bird and owner took a nap together, because the owner thought it would be cute to have the bird sleep with them.

Your birds must be safe when they are out and about. Put away anything a curious bird could get into.

Other owners would call, wanting someone to listen to their confession of accidentally stepping on a treasured pet or closing her in the refrigerator, freezer, washer, or dryer. Fortunately, in the case of the appliances, the bird's disappearance was usually noted before any damage was done.

Marathon cooking sessions may result in overheated cookware or stovetop drip pans, which could kill your bird if the cookware or drip pans are coated with a nonstick finish. As it burns, toxic fumes are released that can kill a beloved pet bird. You may want to consider replacing your nonstick cookware

Bad Plants, Good Plants

Common houseplants can pose a threat to your pet's health. Here are some plants that are considered poisonous to parrots:

- Amaryllis
- Calla lily
- Daffodil
- Dieffenbachia
- English ivy
- Foxglove
- Holly
- Lily-of-the-valley
- Mistletoe
- Rhubarb

What's a parakeet owner to do? Are there any safe plants you can keep in your home without endangering your feathered friend? Fortunately, there are. Some plants that are safe for bird owners to have in their homes include:

- African violets
- Aloe
- Burro's tail
- Christmas cactus
- Edible fig
- Ferns
- Gardenia
- Grape ivy

with stainless steel pots and pans, which you can treat with a nonstick cooking spray to make cleanups safe and easy. By the same token, the self-cleaning cycle on some ovens can create harmful fumes for pet birds. Use this cycle only if you have opened the windows around your bird's cage to let in fresh air. (Make sure your parakeet's cage is closed securely before opening a window.)

Chapter 5

Everyday Care

A parakeet requires care every day to ensure his health and well-being. Birds are happiest when they are secure and comfortable in a safe environment. You can help your parakeet feel more secure by establishing a daily routine and performing the same rituals at around the same time every day. This way, your parakeet knows his needs will be met by the people he considers to be his family. Here are some of the things you'll need to do every single day for your pet:

- Observe your bird for any changes in his behavior or routine. Report any changes to your avian veterinarian immediately.
- Offer fresh food and remove old food. Wash the food dish thoroughly with detergent and water. Rinse thoroughly and allow the dish to air dry.
- Remove the water dish and replace with a clean dish full of fresh water. Wash the soiled dish thoroughly with detergent and water.
- Change the paper in the cage tray.
- Let the bird out of his cage for supervised playtime.

Finally, you'll need to cover your bird's cage at about the same time every night to indicate bedtime. When you cover the cage, you'll probably hear your bird rustling around for a bit, perhaps getting a drink of water or a last mouthful of seeds before settling in for the night. Keep in mind that your parakeet will require eight to ten hours of sleep a day, but you can expect that he will take naps during the day to supplement his nightly snooze.

Be Alert to Health Indicators

Although it may seem a bit unpleasant to discuss, your bird's droppings require daily monitoring because they can tell you a lot about his general health. Parakeets will produce small, flat droppings that appear white in the center with a dark green edge. These droppings are usually composed of equal amounts of fecal material (the green edge), urine (the clear liquid portion), and urates (the white or cream-colored center). A healthy parakeet generally eliminates between twenty-five and fifty times a day, although your bird may go more or less often.

Texture and consistency, along with frequency or lack of droppings, can let you know how your pet is feeling. For instance, if a bird eats a lot of fruits and vegetables, his droppings are generally looser and more watery than a bird who primarily eats seeds. But watery droppings can also indicate illness, such as diabetes or kidney problems, which causes a bird to drink more water than usual.

The color of the droppings can also be an indication of health. Birds who have psittacosis typically have bright lime-green droppings, while healthy birds have avocado or darker green and white droppings. Birds with liver problems may produce droppings that are yellowish or reddish, while birds who have internal bleeding will produce dark, tarry droppings.

A color change doesn't necessarily indicate poor health. For instance, birds who eat pelleted diets tend to have darker droppings than their seed-eating companions, while parrots who have gorged on a particular fresh food soon have droppings with that characteristic color. Birds who overindulge on beets, for instance, produce bright red droppings that can look as though the bird has suffered some serious internal injury. Birds who overdo it on sweet potatoes, blueberries, or raspberries produce orange, blue, or red droppings. During pomegranate season, birds who enjoy this fruit develop violet droppings that can look alarming to an unprepared owner.

Put fresh paper in the cage tray every day. Before you throw the old paper out, take a look at your bird's droppings and make sure nothing looks or smells unusual.

Cleaning the Cage

Cage cleaning should be part of your weekly care routine. Here's how to do it.

- Remove your bird and all cage accessories before cleaning the cage.
- Wipe off (or scrape off) old food from the cage bars and the corners of the cage.
- Place the empty cage in the shower stall and turn on the shower. Running hot water over the cage helps loosen stuck-on food and other debris. Scrub the cage with a toothbrush or other stiff-bristled small brush to loosen anything that remains on the cage after it's been in the shower.
- Once all the debris has been removed, disinfect the cage with a bird-safe spray-on disinfectant that you can buy at a pet supply store. Let the disinfectant remain on the cage bars as directed by the instructions on the bottle, then rinse thoroughly to remove the disinfectant from the cage.
- Dry the cage completely. While the cage is drying, clean the perches and accessories.
- Scrape and wash the perches to keep them clean and free of debris. (Sand the perches with coarse-grain sandpaper from time to time to improve traction for your pet.) Replace perches that are very chewed or cannot be cleaned.
- Rotate the toys in the cage to keep your parakeet's environment interesting. To protect your bird's health, discard toys that are broken, frayed, or worn.
- When the cage is completely dry, replace the accessories and put your bird back into his newly cleaned home.
- Clean the playgym the same way you cleaned the cage.

As part of your daily cage cleaning and observation of your feathered friend, look at his droppings carefully. Learn what is normal for your bird in terms of color, consistency, and frequency, and report any changes to your avian veterinarian promptly.

Seasonal Needs

Warm weather requires a little extra vigilance on your part to make sure your parakeet remains comfortable. To help keep your pet cool, keep him out of direct sun, offer him lots of fresh, juicy vegetables and fruits (be sure to remove these fresh foods from the cage promptly to keep your bird from eating spoiled food), and mist him lightly with a clean spray bottle filled with water only. Use this bottle only for misting your bird.

You must also pay attention to your parakeet's needs when the weather turns cooler. You may want to use a heavier cage cover, especially if you lower the heat in your home at night, or move the bird's cage to another location in your home that is warmer and/or less drafty.

> **CAUTION**
>
> **Warm Weather Warning**
>
> On a warm day, you may notice your bird sitting with his wings held away from his body, rolling his tongue and holding his mouth open. This is how a bird cools himself off. Watch your bird carefully on warm days because he can overheat quickly and may suffer heatstroke, which requires veterinary care. If you live in a warm climate, ask your avian veterinarian how you can protect your bird from this potentially serious problem.

Traveling with Your Bird

When I worked for *Bird Talk*, we often heard from bird owners who wanted to take their pets on vacation and people relocating to another state or country. The advice we gave them about traveling with their bird depended on the owner and their pet. These were some of the questions we asked:

Does the bird like new adventures?

Is there a trusted relative or friend you can leave the bird with while you are away?

Does your avian veterinarian's office offer boarding?

How long will you be gone?

Will you be visiting a foreign country?

Holiday Precautions

The holidays bring their own special set of stresses, and they can also be hazardous to your parakeet's health. Drafts from frequently opening and closing doors can affect your bird's health, and the bustle of a steady stream of visitors can add to your pet's stress level (as well as your own).

Chewing on holiday plants, such as poinsettia, holly, and mistletoe, can make your bird sick, as can chewing on tinsel and ornaments. Round jingle-type bells can sometimes trap a curious bird's toe, beak, or tongue, so keep these holiday decorations out of your bird's reach. Watch your pet around strings of lights, too, as both the bulbs and the cords can be great temptations to curious beaks.

In warm weather, your bird will benefit from regular misting with water.

If the owners were going on a family vacation, we usually recommended leaving the bird at home in familiar surroundings with his own food, water, and cage or in the care of a trusted friend, relative, pet sitter, or avian veterinarian. We advised this because birds are creatures of habit who like their routines, and because taking birds across state lines or international boundaries is not without risk. Some species are illegal in certain states (Quaker, or monk, parakeets, for example, are believed to pose an agricultural threat to some states because of their hearty appetites), and some foreign countries have lengthy quarantine stays for pet birds. It was our professional opinion that, although it is difficult to leave your bird behind when you travel, it is better for the bird. (Of course, if you're moving, that's a different story!)

If you leave your pet at home while you're away, you have several care options available. First, you can recruit the services of a trusted friend or relative, which is an inexpensive and convenient solution for many pet owners. You can return the pet-sitting favor for your friend or relative when they go out of town.

If your trusted friends and relatives live far away, you can hire a professional pet sitter (many advertise in the Yellow Pages, and some offer additional services, such as picking up mail, watering your plants, and leaving on lights and/or radios to make your home seem occupied while you're gone). If

Some birds like to travel, but most are homebodies and prefer familiar surroundings.

you're not sure about what to look for in a pet sitter, the National Association of Professional Pet Sitters offers the following tips.

- Look for a bonded pet sitter who carries commercial liability insurance.
- Ask for references and for a written description of services and fees.
- Arrange to have the pet sitter come to your home before you leave on your trip to meet the pets and discuss what services you would like them to perform while you're away.
- During the initial interview, evaluate the sitter. Do they seem comfortable with your bird? Does the sitter have experience caring for birds? Do they own birds?
- Ask for a written contract and discuss the availability of vet care (whether they have an existing arrangement with your veterinarian, for example) and what arrangements the sitter makes in the event of inclement weather or personal illness.
- Discuss the sitter's policy for making sure you have returned home. Should you call them to confirm your arrival, or will they call you?

If the prospect of leaving your bird with a pet sitter doesn't appeal to you, you may be able to board your bird at your avian veterinarian's office. Of course, you'll need to find out if your vet's office offers boarding services and decide if you want to risk your bird's health by exposing him to other birds during boarding.

Chapter 6

Feeding Your Parakeet

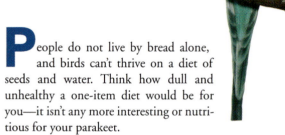

People do not live by bread alone, and birds can't thrive on a diet of seeds and water. Think how dull and unhealthy a one-item diet would be for you—it isn't any more interesting or nutritious for your parakeet.

Poor diet also causes a number of health problems (respiratory infections, poor feather condition, flaky skin, reproductive problems, to name a few) and is one of the main reasons some parakeets live fairly short lives. Let's look again at my childhood pet, who ate basically a seed-and-water diet and lived about five years. We fed him what the people at the pet store told us to feed him, which was what people did thirty years ago. However, if we had offered him a more varied diet and worked with him consistently to accept new foods, Charlie could have lived three times longer.

A Healthy Diet

Here's what the Association of Avian Veterinarians recommends as a healthy parakeet diet: 50 percent seeds, grains, and legumes; 45 percent dark green or dark orange vegetables and fruits; and 5 percent protein in the form of meat (well cooked, please), eggs (also well cooked), or dairy products. We'll look at each part of this diet in a little more detail in just a moment.

Whatever healthy fresh foods you offer your parakeet, be sure to remove any leftover food from the cage promptly to prevent spoilage and to help keep your bird healthy. Ideally, you should change the food in your bird's cage every two to four hours (about every thirty minutes in warm weather), so a parakeet should be all right with a tray of food to pick through in the morning, another to select from during the afternoon, and a fresh salad to nibble on for dinner.

Seeds, Grains, and Legumes

The seeds, grains, and legumes portion of your parakeet's diet can include clean, fresh seed from your local pet supply store. Give your pet her seeds in a clean, dry dish, and check the dish daily to ensure your parakeet has enough food. Don't just look in the dish, but actually remove it from the cage and blow lightly into the dish (you might want to do this over the kitchen sink or the trash can) to remove seed hulls. Parakeets are notorious for giving the impression that they have enough food when they really don't. Because they are such neat eaters and drop the used hulls right back in their dishes, they can often fool you.

One foodstuff that is very popular with parakeets is millet, especially millet sprays. These golden sprays are part treat and part toy. Offer your parakeet this treat sparingly, however, because it is high in fat and can make your parakeet pudgy!

Other items in the bread group that you can offer your pet include unsweetened breakfast cereals, whole-wheat bread, cooked beans, cooked rice, and cooked pasta. Offer a few flakes of cereal at a time, serve small bread cubes, and parakeet-sized portions of rice, beans, or pasta.

Your Parakeet's Beak

Because parakeets eat primarily seeds and other plant materials in the wild (some parakeets have been seen eating the seeds of twenty-one different species of grasses), their beaks have developed into efficient little seed crackers. Look at the underside of your bird's upper beak. It has tiny ridges in it that help your parakeet hold and crack seeds more easily.

How Fresh Are Those Seeds?

You can test seeds for freshness by sprouting some of them in water on your windowsill. Soak the seeds thoroughly in water and drain the excess. In two or three days, fresh seeds will sprout; stale seeds won't. After the fresh seeds sprout, you can rinse them well and feed them to your parakeets, too. Immediately discard any sprouts that smell funny or grow mold; these are unhealthy to feed to your parakeet.

Fruits and Vegetables

Dark green and dark orange vegetables and fruits contain vitamin A, which is an important part of a bird's diet and is missing from the seeds, grains, and legumes. This vitamin helps fight off infection and keeps a bird's eyes, mouth, and respiratory system healthy. Some foods that are rich in vitamin A include carrots, yams, sweet potatoes, broccoli, dried red peppers, dandelion greens, and spinach.

Serve fresh fruits and vegetables to your bird by slicing them into small, parakeet-sized pieces. Shred or julienne carrots and steam or bake yams and sweet potatoes. (Make sure they are cool enough to eat before serving.)

You may be wondering whether to offer frozen or canned vegetables and fruits to your bird. Some birds will eat frozen vegetables and fruits, while others turn their beaks up at the somewhat mushy texture of these foodstuffs. The high sodium

Fresh fruits and vegetables are an important part of a healthy parakeet's diet. Carrot greens and Swiss chard offer plenty of vitamin A.

content in some canned foods may make them unhealthy for your parakeet. Frozen and canned foods will serve your bird's needs in an emergency, but I would offer only fresh foods as a regular part of her diet.

Protein

Along with small portions of well-cooked meat, as I mentioned earlier, you can also offer your parakeet bits of tofu, water-packed tuna, fully cooked scrambled eggs, cottage cheese, unsweetened yogurt, or low-fat cheese. Don't overdo the dairy products,

though, because a bird's digestive system lacks the enzyme lactase, which means your bird's system cannot fully process dairy foods.

Don't Feed These to Your Bird!

Do not feed your pet parakeet alcohol, rhubarb, or avocado (the skin and the area around the pit can be toxic). Don't give her any foods that are highly salted, sweetened, or fatty. Especially do not give your bird chocolate because it contains the chemical theobromine, which birds cannot digest as completely as people can. Chocolate can kill your parakeet, so resist the temptation to share this snack with her. Also avoid giving your bird the seeds or pits from apples, apricots, cherries, peaches, pears, and plums, because they contain toxins that can be harmful to her health.

Sharing People Food

Let common sense be your guide in choosing which foods you can share with your bird: If it's healthy for you, it's probably okay to share. However, remember to reduce the size of the portion you offer to your bird—a few shreds of grated carrot or squash, a single Cheerio, or a few cooked beans will be more appealing to your parakeet than a larger, human-sized portion.

It's fine to feed your bird healthy people food, such as cooked pasta. Just don't offer her anything you have already taken a bite from.

Sharing healthy people food with your parakeet is completely acceptable, but sharing something that you've already taken a bite of is not. Human saliva has bacteria in it that are perfectly normal for people but are potentially toxic to birds, so please don't share partially eaten food with your pet. For your bird's health and your peace of mind, give her a separate portion.

By the same token, please don't kiss your parakeet on the beak (kiss her on top of her little head instead) or allow your parakeet to put her head into your mouth, nibble on your lips, or preen your teeth. Although you may see birds doing this on television or in pictures in a magazine and think it's a cute trick, it's really unsafe for your bird's health and well-being.

The Pelleted Diet Option

You're probably wondering just what a pellet is. Don't birds eat seeds? While seeds are an important part of many birds' diets, some parakeet owners prefer to feed their pets a pelleted diet rather than a mixture of seeds, vegetables, fruits, and healthful table food.

Pelleted diets are created by mixing a variety of nutritious ingredients into a mash and then forcing (or extruding) the hot mixture through a machine to form various shapes. Some pelleted diets have colors and flavors added, while others are fairly plain. These formulated diets provide more balanced nutrition for your pet bird in an easy-to-serve form that reduces the amount of wasted food and eliminates the chance for a bird to pick through a smorgasbord of healthy foods to find her favorites and reject the foods she isn't particularly fond of. Some parakeets accept pelleted diets quickly, while others require some persuading.

Introducing New Foods

If you have adopted an older parakeet who eats primarily seeds, try offering your bird some of the fruits and vegetables that are popular with many parrots, such as apple slices, grapes, and corn. You can offer a small slice of apple that you've dipped in seeds, half a grape, or some fresh corn kernels (offering a thin "wheel" of corn on the cob is also an option). Although these fruits and vegetables are not as rich in important vitamins as their dark green and dark orange counterparts, they can help bridge the gap between seeds and a more varied diet for fussy eaters.

To ease the stress of relocating to your home, try to feed your parakeet a diet as close to the one she ate in her previous home. To help your bird adjust even faster, you may want to sprinkle some food on the cage floor, because parakeets sometimes revert to their natural ground-feeding habits in times of stress.

If your parakeet seems a bit finicky about trying pellets, you may have to make her believe that you enjoy pellets as a snack. Really play up your apparent enjoyment of this new food, because it will pique your parakeet's curiosity and make the pellets exceedingly interesting.

If you have another bird in the house who already eats a pelleted diet, place your parakeet's cage where she can watch the other bird enjoy her pellets. Before long, your parakeet will be playing "follow the leader" right to the food bowl. Finally, you may want to roll a favorite treat, such as a damp broccoli floret or an apple slice, in pellets and offer this decorated piece of produce to your pet.

Whatever you do, don't starve your bird into trying a new food. Offer a variety of new foods consistently, along with familiar favorites. This will ensure that your bird is eating and will also encourage her to try new foods. Don't be discouraged if your parakeet doesn't dive right in to a new food. Be patient, keep offering new foods to your bird, and praise her enthusiastically when she is brave enough to sample something new!

If you want to convert your pet to a pelleted diet, you need to offer her pellets alongside or mixed with her current diet. Once you see that your bird is eating the pellets, begin to gradually increase the amount of pellets you offer at mealtime while decreasing the amount of other food you serve. Within a couple of weeks, your bird should be eating her pellets with gusto!

Grit

As a new bird owner, you may hear a lot of talk about the importance of grit in your bird's diet. Birds use grit in their gizzard to grind their food, much as we use our teeth. Avian veterinarians and bird breeders do not agree on how much grit birds need and how often it should be offered to them. Some will tell you birds need grit regularly while others will advise against it.

If your parakeet's breeder and your avian veterinarian think your bird needs grit, offer it sparingly (only about a pinch every few weeks). Do not offer it daily and do not provide your parakeet with a separate dish of grit because some birds will overeat the grit and suffer dangerous crop impactions as a result.

Supplements

You may also be concerned about whether your bird is getting enough vitamins and minerals in her diet. This is of particular concern if your parakeet is eating a seed-based diet. Parakeets on pelleted diets should be getting all the vitamins and minerals they need from these special diets, so supplements are unnecessary. If your parakeet's diet is mainly seeds, however, you may want to sprinkle a good-quality vitamin and mineral powder onto your pet's fresh foods, where it has the best chance of sticking to the food and being eaten. Vitamin-enriched seed diets may provide some supplementation, but some brands add the vitamins and minerals to the seed hull, which your pet will remove and discard while she's eating.

Avoid adding vitamin and mineral supplements to your parakeet's water dish, because they can act as a growth medium for bacteria. They may also cause the water to taste different to your bird, which could discourage her from drinking.

CAUTION

Diet Taboos

Here's a little list to help you remember what foods to avoid:

Alcohol

Avocado

Candy

Chocolate

Potato chips

Pretzels

Rhubarb

Seeds or pits from apples, apricots, cherries, peaches, pears, and plums

What About Water?

In addition to providing fresh food every day, you must give your bird access to clean, fresh water daily. Birds require water to digest their food properly and to maintain good health, and their drinking water should be offered separately from any water they use to bathe.

If you choose to add a vitamin and mineral supplement to your bird's diet, offer it along with her fresh food.

Some parakeets prefer to drink from open dishes, while others like to drink from water bottles. Find out which type of water container your bird is accustomed to before you bring her home, so she'll know right away where to look when she's thirsty!

Chapter 7

Grooming Your Parakeet

Your parakeet must be able to bathe regularly, and he will need to have his nails and flight feathers trimmed periodically to ensure his safety.

Although some people would say a parakeet's beak also needs trimming, I believe a healthy bird who has enough chew toys seems to do a remarkable job of keeping his beak trimmed all on his own. If your parakeet's beak becomes overgrown, though, please consult your avian veterinarian. A parrot's beak contains a surprising number of blood vessels, so beak trimming is best left to the experts. Also, a suddenly overgrown beak may indicate that your bird is suffering from liver damage, a virus, or scaly mites, all of which require veterinary care.

Preening

Preening is one of your parakeet's ways of keeping himself well groomed. You will notice him ruffling and straightening his feathers each day. He will also take oil from the gland at the base of his tail and spread it on the rest of his feathers, so don't be concerned if you see your parakeet apparently pecking or biting at his tail. Preening, combined with your assistance in bathing and nail and wing clipping, will keep your parakeet in top shape.

Bathing

You can bathe your parakeet in a variety of ways. You can mist him lightly with a clean spray bottle filled with warm water (and *only* warm water), or you can allow him to bathe in the kitchen or bathroom sink under a slow stream of water. Many parakeets prefer to bathe in their cages, either in a small, flat saucer of warm water, a plastic parakeet bathtub, or an enclosed birdbath that you can buy in your local pet supply store. Bathing is important to birds to help them keep their feathers clean and healthy, so don't deny your pet the chance to bathe!

Some parakeets combine bathing with mealtime by rolling around in damp, fresh greens provided by their owners. Offer your parakeet an opportunity to do this by providing the tops from beets or carrots or a leaf of lettuce (not iceberg, please—it doesn't contain any nutrients) for him to play with. He will bathe indirectly as the water from the greens falls onto his feathers.

Unless your parakeet has gotten himself into oil, paint, wax, or some other substance that plain water alone won't remove and that could harm his feathers, he will not require soap as part of his bath. Under routine conditions, soaps and detergents can damage a bird's feathers by removing beneficial oils, so hold the shampoo during your parakeet's normal cleanup.

Let your bird bathe early in the day so his feathers have an opportunity to dry completely during the day. In cooler weather, you may want to help the process along by drying your parakeet off with a blow dryer to prevent him from becoming chilled after his bath. To do this, set the blow dryer on low and keep it moving so that your bird doesn't become overheated. Your parakeet may soon learn that drying off is the most enjoyable part of his bath!

Preening is your bird's way of keeping himself beautifully groomed.

Nail Trimming

You must look after the health of your bird's nails and beak. You can trim the nails yourself, but if beak trimming is necessary (and usually it isn't), that's a job for your avian veterinarian..

Parakeets and other parrots need their nails clipped occasionally to keep the nails from catching on toys or perches and injuring themselves. Trimming your parakeet's nails is a fairly simple procedure. Unlike some of the larger parrots, a parakeet's nails are light in color, which makes it easier for you to see where the nail stops and the blood supply (called the quick) begins. In parakeets, the quick is generally seen as a pink line or area inside the nail.

You need to remove only tiny portions of the nail to keep your parakeet's claws trimmed. Generally, a good guideline is to remove only the hook on each nail and to do this in the smallest increments possible. Stop well before you reach the quick. If you do happen to cut the nail short enough to make it bleed, apply cornstarch or flour, followed by direct pressure, to stop the bleeding.

Wing Trimming

The goal of a proper wing trim is to prevent your pet from flying away or flying into a window, mirror, or wall while he's out of his cage. An added benefit is that his inability to fly well will make him more dependent on you for transportation, which should make him easier to handle. However, the bird still needs enough wing feathers so that he can glide safely to the ground if he is startled and takes flight from his cage top or playgym.

Because this is a delicate procedure, I strongly recommend that you enlist the help of your avian veterinarian, at least the first time, so you are clear about what to do and how to do it. Wing trimming is a task that must be performed carefully to avoid injuring your pet, so take your time if you're doing it yourself. Please do not just take up the largest pair of kitchen shears you own and start snipping away, because I have had avian veterinarians tell me about parakeets whose owners cut off their birds' wing tips (down to the bone) in this manner.

Clip the flight feathers on the outside of the wing, so they are even with the covert feathers (which are above them).

You'll find step-by-step instructions on how to trim your bird's wings on pages 64–65. I encourage you to groom your pet in a quiet, well-lit place because grooming excites some birds and causes them to become wiggly. Having good light to work under will make your job easier, and having a quiet work area may calm down your pet and make him a bit easier to handle.

Molting

At least once a year, your parakeet will lose his feathers. Don't be alarmed, because this is a normal process called molting. I say "at least once" because many pet birds seem to be in a perpetual molt, with feathers falling out and coming in throughout the summer.

You can consider your bird to be in molting season when you see a lot of whole feathers in the bottom of the cage and you notice that your bird seems to have broken out in a rash of stubbly little aglets (those plastic tips on the ends of your shoelaces). These are the feather sheaths that help new pinfeathers break through the skin, and they are made of keratin (the same material that makes up our fingernails). The sheaths help protect growing feathers from damage until the feathers complete their growth cycle.

You may notice that your parakeet is a little more irritable during the molt; this is to be expected. Think about how you would feel if you had all these itchy new feathers coming in all of a sudden. However, your bird may actively seek out more time with you during the molt because an owner is handy to have

Wing Trimming Step by Step

The first step in trimming your parakeet's wing feathers is to assemble all the things you will need and find a quiet, well-lit place to groom your pet before you catch and trim him. Your grooming tools will include:

- Washcloth or small towel to wrap your parakeet in
- Small, sharp scissors to do the actual trimming
- Needle-nosed pliers (to pull out any blood feathers you may cut accidentally)
- Flour or cornstarch (not styptic powder) to stop the bleeding in case a blood feather is cut
- Nail trimmers (while you have your bird wrapped in the towel, you might as well do his nails, too)

Once you've assembled your supplies and found a quiet grooming location, drape the towel over your hand and catch your parakeet with your toweled hand. Gently grab your bird by the back of his head and neck (never compress the chest) and wrap him in the towel—firmly enough to hold him but not too tight! Hold your bird's head securely through the towel with your thumb and index finger. (Having the bird's head covered by the towel will calm him and will give him something to chew on while you clip his wings.)

Lay the bird on his back, being careful not to constrict or compress his chest (remember, birds have no diaphragms to help them breathe), and spread his wing out carefully. You will see an upper row of short feathers, called the covert feathers, and a lower row of long feathers, which are the flight feathers. Look for new flight feathers that are still growing in, also called blood feathers. These can be identified by their waxy, tight look (new feathers in their feather sheaths resemble the end of a shoelace) and their dark centers or quills—the dark color is caused by the blood supply to the new feather. **Never trim a blood feather.**

If your bird has a number of blood feathers, you may want to put off trimming his wings for a few days, because older, fully grown feathers act as a cushion to protect those just coming in from life's hard knocks. If your bird has only one or two blood feathers, you can trim the full-grown feathers accordingly.

To trim your bird's feathers, separate each one away from the other flight feathers and cut it individually (remember, the goal is to have a well-trimmed bird who is still able to glide a bit if he needs to). Start from the tip of the wing when you trim, and clip just five to eight feathers in. Use the primary covert feathers (the set of feathers above the primary flight feathers) as a guideline as to how short you should trim—trim the flight feathers so they are just a tiny bit longer than the coverts.

Be sure to trim an equal number of feathers from each wing. Although some people think that a bird needs only one trimmed wing, this is incorrect and could actually harm a bird who tries to fly with one trimmed and one untrimmed wing. Think of how off balance that would make you feel; your parakeet is no different.

Now that you've successfully trimmed your bird's wing feathers, congratulate yourself. You've just taken a great step toward keeping your parakeet safe. Now you must remember to check your parakeet's wing feathers and retrim them periodically (about four times a year is a minimum).

Blood Feather First Aid

If you do happen to cut a blood feather, remain calm. You must remove it and stop the bleeding to ensure that your bird doesn't bleed to death, and panicking will do neither of you any good.

To remove a blood feather, use a pair of needle-nosed pliers to grasp the broken feather's shaft as close to the skin of the wing as you can. With one steady motion, pull the feather out completely. After you've removed the feather, put a pinch of flour or cornstarch on the feather follicle (the spot where you pulled out the feather) and apply direct pressure for a few minutes until the bleeding stops. If the bleeding doesn't stop after a few minutes of direct pressure, or if you can't remove the feather shaft, contact your avian veterinarian immediately for further instructions.

Although it may seem like you're hurting your parakeet by removing the broken blood feather, consider this: A broken blood feather is like an open faucet. If left in, the faucet stays open and lets the blood out. Once removed, the bird's skin generally closes up behind the feather shaft and shuts off the faucet.

These birds have trimmed wings, and will not be able to fly away and get lost.

around when a parakeet has an itch on the top of his head that he can't quite scratch! (Scratch these new feathers gently because some of them may still be growing in and may be sensitive to the touch.) Some birds may benefit from special conditioning foods during the molt; check with your avian veterinarian to see if your bird is a candidate for these foods.

Be particularly alert after a molt, because your bird will have a whole new crop of flight feathers that need attention. You'll be able to tell when your parakeet is due for a trim when he starts becoming bolder in his flying attempts. Right after a wing trim, a parakeet generally tries to fly and finds he's unsuccessful at the attempt. He will keep trying, though, and may surprise you one day with a fairly good glide from the top of his cage or playgym. If this happens, get the scissors and trim those wings immediately. If you don't, the section that follows on finding lost birds may have more meaning than you can imagine.

If Your Bird Escapes

Now that we have covered wing trimming, it's as good a time as any to discuss the possibility of your bird escaping. One of the most common accidents that befalls bird owners is a fully flighted bird (one without a wing trim) escaping through an open door or window. Just because your bird has never flown before or shown any interest in leaving his cage doesn't mean that he can't fly or that he won't become disoriented once he's outside. If you don't believe it can happen, just check the lost and found advertisements in your local newspaper for a week. Chances are many birds will turn up in the lost column, but few are ever found.

Why don't lost birds ever come home? Some fall victim to predatory animals in the wild, while others join flocks of feral, or wild, parrots. (Florida and California are particularly noted for these.) Still other lost birds end up miles away from home because they fly wildly and frantically in any direction. And

Keeping Your Bird Safe

How can you prevent your bird from becoming lost? Here are some tips:

- Make sure his wings are safely trimmed at regular intervals.
- Trim both wings evenly and remember to trim them after your bird has molted.
- Make sure your bird's cage door locks securely and that his cage tray cannot come lose if the cage is knocked over or dropped accidentally.
- Check your window screens to be sure they fit securely and are free from tears and holes.
- Keep all window screens and patio doors closed when your bird is at liberty.
- Never go outside with your bird on your shoulder.

the people who find them don't advertise in the same area that the birds were lost in. Finally, some people who find lost birds don't advertise that they've been found because the finders think that whoever was unlucky or uncaring enough to lose the bird in the first place doesn't deserve to have him back.

How to Catch an Escaped Bird

If, despite your best efforts, your bird escapes, you must act quickly for the best chance of recovering your pet. Here are some things to keep in mind:

- If possible, keep the bird in sight. This will make chasing him easier.
- Make an audiotape of your bird's voice (ready for just such an emergency) and play it outside on a portable tape recorder to lure your bird back home.
- Place your bird's cage in an area where he is likely to see it, such as on a deck or patio. Put lots of treats and food on the floor of the cage to tempt your pet back into his home.
- Use another caged bird to attract your parakeet's attention.

- Alert your avian veterinarian's office that your bird has escaped. Also notify the local humane society and other veterinary offices in your area.
- Post fliers in your neighborhood describing your bird. Offer a reward and include your phone number.
- Don't give up hope.

Are Mite Protectors Necessary?

While we're discussing grooming and feather care, I'd like to recommend that you do not purchase mite protectors that hang on a bird's cage or conditioning products that are applied directly to a bird's feathers. Well-cared-for parakeets

don't have mites and shouldn't be in danger of contracting them. (If your pet does have mites, veterinary care is the most effective way to treat them.) Also, the fumes from some of these products are quite strong and can be harmful to your pet's health.

Conditioners, anti-picking products, and other substances that are applied to your bird's feathers will serve one purpose: to get your bird to preen himself so thoroughly in an effort to remove the offending liquid that he could remove all his feathers in a particular area. If you want to encourage your bird to preen regularly and help condition his feathers, simply mist him regularly with clean, warm water or hold him under a gentle stream from a kitchen or bathroom faucet. Your bird will take care of the rest.

Make sure all windows and doors are closed before you let your bird out of his cage. He's safe at home, but pet parakeets are not meant to live in the wild.

Chapter 8

Keeping Your Parakeet Healthy

Avian Anatomy

If you think your body doesn't have much in common with your pet parakeet's, you're wrong. You both have skin; skeletons; respiratory, cardiovascular, digestive, excretory, and nervous systems; and sensory organs, although the various systems function in slightly different ways.

Skin

Your parakeet's skin is probably pretty difficult to see, since she has so many feathers. If you part the feathers carefully, though, you can see your pet's thin, transparent skin and the muscles beneath it. Modified skin cells help make up your bird's beak, cere, claws, and the scales on her feet and legs.

Skeletal System

Next, let's look at your bird's skeleton. Did you know that some bird bones are hollow? This makes them lighter (which makes flying easier), but it also means those bones can break more easily. That's why you must always handle your bird carefully! Another adaptation for flight is that the bones of a bird's wing (which correspond to our arm and hand bones) are fused for greater strength.

Birds have air sacs in some of their bones (these are called pneumatic bones) that help lighten their bodies for flight. They also have air sacs throughout their bodies to cool them more efficiently. Because birds have no sweat glands, they

A parrot has a light and flexible body, which is convenient for preening and scratching.

cannot perspire as mammals do and they must have a different way to cool off.

A parrot has ten neck vertebrae, compared to a human's seven. This makes a parrot's neck more free moving than a person's (a parrot can turn her head almost 180 degrees), which can be advantageous for spotting food or predators in the wild.

During breeding season, a female bird's bones become denser as they store calcium needed to create eggshells. As a result, a female's skeleton can weigh up to 20 percent more during breeding season than it does the rest of the year.

Respiratory System

Your bird's respiratory system is highly efficient and works in a markedly different way from yours. Here's how your parakeet breathes: Air enters the system through your bird's nares, which are passages through her sinuses and into her throat. As it does, the air is filtered through the choana, which is a slit that can easily be seen in the roof of many birds' mouths. The choana also helps clean and warm the air before it goes further into the respiratory system.

After the air passes the choana, it flows through the larynx and trachea, and past the syrinx, or voice box. Your bird doesn't have vocal cords like you do; rather, vibration of the syrinx membrane is what enables birds to make sounds.

So far it sounds similar to the way we breathe, doesn't it? Well, here's where the differences begin. As the air continues its journey past the syrinx and into the bronchi, your bird's lungs don't expand and contract to bring the air in and out. This is partly due to the fact that birds don't have diaphragms, as people do. Instead, the bird's body wall expands and contracts, much like a fireplace bellows. This action brings air into the air sacs I mentioned earlier. The bellows action also moves air in and out of the lungs.

Although a bird's respiratory system is extremely efficient at exchanging gases in the system, two complete breaths are required to do the same work that a single breath does in people and other mammals. This is why you may notice that your bird seems to breathe quite quickly. The average respiratory rate for a parakeet is between sixty-five and eighty-five breaths per minute (compared to the average twelve to sixteen breaths per minute a person takes).

Cardiovascular System

Along with the respiratory system, your bird's cardiovascular system keeps oxygen and other nutrients moving throughout her body, although the circulatory path in your parakeet is different from yours. In your parakeet, blood flowing from the legs, reproductive system, and lower intestines passes through the kidneys on its way back to the general circulatory system.

Like you, though, your parakeet has a four-chambered heart, with two atria and two ventricles. Unlike your average heart rate of seventy-two beats per minute, your parakeet's average heart rate is 350 to 550 beats per minute. Having such an efficient circulatory system enables parakeets and other parrots to use incredible amounts of energy very efficiently.

Digestive System

To keep this energy-efficient machine running requires fuel. That's where your bird's digestive system comes in. One of the main functions of the digestive system is to provide the fuel that maintains your bird's body temperature.

Your parakeet's digestive system begins with her beak. The size and shape of a bird's beak depend on what she eats and how she gathers it. Compare the sharp, pointed beak of an eagle or the elongated bill of a hummingbird with the small, hooked beak of your parakeet.

A parrot's mouth works a little differently than a mammal's. Parrots don't have saliva to help break down and move their food around, the way we do. Instead, after the food leaves your bird's mouth, it travels down the esophagus, where it is moistened. The food then travels to the crop, where it is moistened further and is passed in small increments into the bird's gizzard.

Parrots have few taste buds, and they are located in the roof of the mouth. It's likely they do not have a very refined sense of taste.

Checking the Cage Bottom

Because parakeets come from such a dry environment in the interior of Australia, their droppings are drier than those of other, larger parrots who come from tropical jungle regions. Budgie droppings resemble small green-and-white chips, as opposed to the larger, wetter piles of droppings that bigger birds produce.

Bird droppings consist of three parts:

- The feces, which are the darker, solid portion of the droppings
- The urine, which is the liquid part of the droppings
- The urates, which is the creamy white portion of the droppings seen around the feces

Although bird droppings are probably among the least-appealing parts of owning a pet bird, they are also one of the most important. The size, shape, color, consistency, and frequency of your bird's droppings can indicate health or illness. Any change from your bird's normal elimination routine can also signal health or behavioral problems that may require a veterinary evaluation.

Make it a habit to observe your bird's droppings each day. Does she seem to be eliminating more or less than usual? Are the droppings wetter than normal? Have they changed color? If you notice something out of the ordinary, contact your avian veterinarian's office for an evaluation appointment to ensure your parakeet remains in good health.

Between the crop and the gizzard, food passes through the proventriculus, where digestive juices are added. Once in the gizzard, it is broken down into even smaller pieces.

The food then travels to the small intestine, where nutrients are absorbed into the bloodstream. Anything that's left over then travels through the large intestine to the cloaca, which is the common chamber that collects wastes before they leave the bird's body through the vent. The whole process from mouth to vent usually takes only a few hours, which is why you may notice that your bird leaves frequent, small droppings in her cage.

Along with the solid waste created by the digestive system, your parakeet's kidneys create urine, which is then transported through ureters to the cloaca for excretion. Unlike mammals, birds do not have a bladder or a urethra.

Nervous System

Your parakeet's nervous system is very similar to your own. Both are made up of the brain, the spinal cord, and countless nerves throughout the body that transmit messages to and from the brain.

Feathers

Birds are the only animals that have feathers, and they serve several purposes. Feathers help birds fly, they keep birds warm, they attract the attention of potential mates, and they help scare away predators. Did you know that your parakeet has between 2,000 and 3,000 feathers on her body? These feathers grow from follicles that are arranged in rows known as pterylae. The unfeathered patches of bare skin on your parakeet's body are called apteria.

A feather is a remarkably designed creation. The base of the feather shaft, which fits into the bird's skin, is called the quill. It is light and hollow, but remarkably tough. The upper part of the feather shaft is called the rachis. From it branch the barbs and barbules (smaller barbs) that make up most of the feather. The barbs and barbules have small hooks on them that enable the different parts of the feather to interlock like Velcro and form the feather's vane, or web.

Although you may notice a few bare patches in your bird's feathers during a molt, her body is constantly growing replacement feathers so that she is never completely without the ability to fly. While it grows, a feather has an outer keratin layer that is similar to our fingernails. This keratin layer helps the feather emerge through the bird's skin while it grows, and then the keratin breaks off or is preened off

These long primary flight feathers push a bird forward during flight. They are also the ones that need to be clipped.

by the bird as the new feather takes its place on her body.

Birds have several different types of feathers on their bodies. Contour feathers are the colorful outer feathers on a bird's body and wings. Many birds have an undercoating of down feathers that helps keep them warm. Semiplume feathers are found on a bird's beak, nares (nostrils), and eyelids.

A bird's flight feathers can be classified into one of two types. Primary flight feathers are the large wing feathers that push a bird forward during flight. They are also the ones that need clipping (see chapter 7). Secondary flight feathers are found on the inner wing, and they help support the bird in flight. Primary and secondary wing feathers can operate independently of each other. The bird's tail feathers also assist in flight by acting as brakes and a rudder to make steering easier.

Feather colors are determined by combinations of pigment in the outer layer and in the interior structure of the feather. All parrot species start out in their "wild" color, which is the color their feathers are in their native surroundings. In captive situations, new and unusual colors, called mutations, can occur. In the wild, birds of a different color mutation may be more easily spotted by predators (and eaten before they have a chance to breed and pass that color along to their offspring), but in captivity they can be paired with other different-colored birds to create even more mutations. These color mutations are most often seen in parakeets, cockatiels, lovebirds, Quaker parakeets, ring-necked parakeets, and grass parakeets.

To keep their feathers in good condition, healthy birds will spend a great deal of time fluffing and preening them. You may see your parakeet seeming to pick at the base of her tail on the topside. This is a normal behavior in which the bird removes oil from the preen gland and spreads it on her feathers. The oil also helps prevent skin infections and waterproofs the feathers.

Sometimes pet birds will develop white lines or small holes on the large feathers of their wings and tails. These lines or holes are called stress bars or stress lines, and result from the bird experiencing stress as the feathers were developing. If you notice stress bars on your parakeet's feathers, discuss them with your avian veterinarian.

Parakeet Senses

Sight

Although I mentioned earlier that a bird has a poor sense of taste, she has a well-developed sense of sight. Birds can see detail and they can discern colors. Be aware of this when your are selecting cage accessories for your pet, because some parakeets react to a change in the color of their food dishes. Some seem excited by a different color bowl, while others act fearful of the new item.

Because their eyes are located on the sides of their heads, most pet birds rely on monocular vision, which means they use each eye independently of the other. If a bird really wants to study an object, you will often see her tilt her head to one side and examine the object with just one eye. Birds aren't really able to move their eyes around very much, but they compensate for this by having highly mobile necks that enable them to turn their heads about 180 degrees.

Like cats and dogs, birds have a third eyelid called the nictitating membrane that you will sometimes see flick briefly across your parakeet's eye. The purpose of this membrane is to keep the eyeball moist and clean. If you see your parakeet's nictitating membrane for more than a brief second, please contact your avian veterinarian for an evaluation.

You have probably noticed that your bird lacks eyelashes. In their place are small feathers called semi-plumes that help keep dirt and dust out of the bird's eyeballs.

Hearing

You may be wondering where your parakeet's ears are. Look carefully under the feathers behind and below each eye to find them. The ears are the somewhat large holes in the sides of your parakeet's head. Parakeets have about the same ability to distinguish sound waves and determine the location of the sound as people do, but birds seem to be less sensitive to higher and lower pitches than their owners.

Each eye functions independently, so a bird will often title her head from side to side to study something carefully.

Parrots have two toes that point forward and two that point backward. This enables them to climb and also to manipulate objects.

Taste and Smell

How do your parakeet's senses of smell and taste compare to your own? Birds seem to have poorly developed senses of smell and taste because smells often dissipate quickly in the air (where flying birds spend their time) and because birds have fewer taste buds in their mouths than people do. Also, their taste buds are contained in the roofs of their mouths (not in the tongue, as ours are). Experts think a parrot's sense of taste is poorly developed.

Touch

The final sense we relate to, touch, is well developed in parrots. Parrots use their feet and their mouths to touch their surroundings (young birds, particularly, seem to "mouth" everything they can get their beaks on), to play, and to determine what is safe to perch on or chew on and what's good to eat.

Along with their tactile uses, a parrot's feet also have an unusual design compared to other caged birds. Look at your parakeet's feet and compare them to the feet of a finch or canary. Do you notice that, unlike a finch or canary, two of your parakeet's toes point forward and two point backward? This arrangement is called zygodactyl, and it enables a parrot to easily climb up and down and around in trees. Some larger parrots also use their feet to hold food or to play with toys.

Visiting the Veterinarian

With good care, a parakeet can live up to eighteen years, although the average life span of these small parrots is about one-third of that, or six years. One of the reasons parakeets don't live longer is that their owners may be reluctant to take their pets to the veterinarian. Some people don't want to pay veterinary bills for such "inexpensive" birds.

Choosing an Avian Veterinarian

As a caring owner, you want your bird to have good care and the best chance to live a long, healthy life. To that end, you will need to find a veterinarian who understands the special medical needs of birds and one with whom you can establish a good working relationship. The best time to do this is when you first bring your parakeet home from the breeder or pet store. If possible, arrange to visit your veterinarian's office on your way home from the breeder or store. This is particularly important if you have other birds at home, because you don't want to endanger the health of your existing flock or your new pet.

If you don't know an avian veterinarian in your area, ask the person from whom you bought your parakeet where they take their birds. (Breeders and bird stores usually have avian veterinarians on whom they depend.) Talk to other bird owners you know and find out whom they take their pets to, or call bird clubs in your area for referrals.

If you have no bird-owning friends or can't locate a bird club, your next best bet is the Yellow Pages. Read the advertisements for veterinarians carefully and try to find one who specializes in birds. Many veterinarians who have an interest in treating birds will join the Association of Avian Veterinarians and advertise themselves as members of this organization. Some veterinarians have taken and passed a special examination that entitles them to call themselves avian specialists.

Once you've received your recommendations or found likely candidates in the telephone book, start calling the veterinary offices. Ask the receptionist how many birds the doctor sees in a week or month, how much an office visit costs, and what payment options are available (cash, credit card, check, or time payments). You can also inquire if the doctor keeps birds as pets.

When it's time to go to the vet, your bird needs to see an avian specialist. Veterinarians who regularly treat cats and dogs are not familiar with the special medical needs of birds.

Signs of Illness

To help your veterinarian and to protect your pet from long-term health problems, keep a close eye on her daily activities and appearance. If something suddenly changes in the way your bird looks or acts, contact your veterinarian immediately. Birds naturally hide signs of illness to protect themselves from predators, so by the time a bird looks or acts sick, she may already be dangerously ill.

Some signs of illness include:

- A fluffed-up appearance
- Loss of appetite
- Sleeping all the time
- A change in the appearance or number of droppings
- Weight loss
- Listlessness
- Drooping wings
- Lameness
- Partially eaten food stuck to the face or food has been regurgitated onto the cage floor
- Labored breathing, with or without tail bobbing
- Runny eyes or nose
- Stops talking or singing

If your bird shows any of these signs, please contact your veterinarian's office immediately.

If you like the answers you receive from the receptionist, make an appointment for your parakeet to be evaluated. (If you don't, of course, move on to the next name on your list.) Make a list of any questions you want to ask the doctor regarding your bird's diet, how often your bird's wings and nails should be clipped, how often you should bring the bird in for an examination, and anything else you feel you need to know.

Plan to arrive a little early for your first appointment because you will be asked to fill out a patient information form. This form will ask you for your bird's name, her age and sex, the length of time you have owned her, your name, address, and telephone number, your preferred method of paying for veterinary services, how you heard about the veterinary office, and the name and address of a friend the veterinary office can contact in case of emergency. The form may also ask you to express your opinion on the amount of money you would spend on your pet in an emergency, because this can help the doctor know what kind of treatment to recommend in such instances.

What the Veterinarian May Ask You

Do not be afraid to ask your avian veterinarians questions. Avian vets have devoted a lot of time, energy, and effort to studying birds, so put this resource to use whenever you can.

You may also be asked a number of questions by the veterinarian. These may include:

- Why is the bird here today?
- What is the bird's normal activity level?
- How is the bird's appetite?
- What does the bird's normal diet consist of?
- Have you noticed a change in the bird's appearance lately?

Be sure to explain any changes in as much detail as you can, because changes in your bird's normal behavior can indicate illness.

During the initial examination, the veterinarian will probably take the first look at your parakeet while she is still in her cage or carrier. The doctor may talk to you and your bird for a few minutes to give the bird an opportunity to become accustomed to them, rather than simply reaching right in and grabbing your pet. While the veterinarian is talking to you, they will check the bird's posture and her ability to perch.

Next, the doctor should remove the bird from her carrier or cage and look her over carefully. They will particularly note the condition of your pet's eyes, her beak, and her

The avian vet will carefully note the condition of your parakeet's eyes, beak, and nares

nares. The bird should be weighed, and the veterinarian will probably palpate (feel) your parakeet's body and wings for any lumps, bumps, or deformities that require further investigation. Feather condition will also be assessed, as will the condition of the bird's vent, legs, and feet.

Once the examination is concluded and you've had a chance to discuss any questions you have with your veterinarian, the doctor will probably recommend a follow-up examination schedule for your pet. Most healthy birds visit the veterinarian annually, but some need to go more frequently.

Medicating Your Parakeet

Most bird owners are faced with the prospect of medicating their pets at some point in the birds' lives, and many are not sure if they can complete the task without hurting their pets. If you have to medicate your pet, your avian veterinarian or veterinary technician should explain the process to you. In the course of the explanation, you should find out how you will be administering the medication, how much of the drug you will be giving your bird, how often the bird needs the medication, and how long the entire course of treatment will last.

If you find (as I often have) that you've forgotten one or more of these steps after you arrive home, call your vet's office for clarification to make sure your bird receives the follow-up care from you that she needs.

I know from personal experience that all the methods I will describe here do work and are survivable by both bird and owner.

Oral Medication

This is a good route to take with birds who are small, easy to handle, or underweight. The medication is usually given with a plastic syringe, minus the needle, placed in the left side of the bird's mouth and pointed toward the right side of her throat. This route is recommended to ensure that the medication gets into the bird's digestive system and not into her lungs, where aspiration pneumonia can result.

Medicating a bird's food or offering medicated feed is another effective possibility, but medications added to a bird's water supply are often less effective because sick birds are less likely to drink water, and the medicated water may have an unusual taste that makes the bird less likely to drink it.

Alternative Health Treatments

Homeopathic treatments, herbal remedies, and acupuncture have become commonplace alternative medical treatments for people today, but did you know they can also be used to treat pet birds? Veterinarians began investigating alternative health treatments for pets in the 1980s, and today pet bird owners may be able to choose such treatments for their birds.

Birds may be good candidates for alternative medical treatments because of their physical and emotional makeup. Their natures are well suited to a holistic approach, which takes into account the bird's whole environment and routine when evaluating her health or illness. A bird owner who practices a holistic approach to bird care will carefully evaluate their bird daily for signs of illness while feeding her a top-quality diet and ensuring that the bird has an interesting and varied routine each day. If something is out of the ordinary during the owner's daily evaluation, they contact an avian veterinarian for an appointment as soon as the change is noted, rather than waiting to see what might happen to the bird.

Look in the yellow pages for veterinarians in your area who include holistic or alternative treatments in their practice, and call the office to find out whether the doctor treats birds. If you don't have a holistic veterinarian in your area, discuss alternative treatment options with your avian veterinarian to see if they are an option for your parakeet when she is ill or injured.

Injected Medication

Avian veterinarians consider this the most effective method of medicating birds. Some injection sites—into a vein, beneath the skin, or into a bone—are used by avian veterinarians in the clinic. Bird owners are usually asked to medicate their birds intramuscularly by injecting medication into the bird's chest muscle. This is the area of the bird's body that has the greatest muscle mass, so it is a good injection site.

It's perfectly understandable if you're hesitant about giving your bird shots. I was the first time I had to medicate a bird this way, but we both survived the

Hold your bird securely on her back to give her medication; don't hold her across the chest. Talk to her calmly and in a soothing voice.

procedure. Wrap your bird securely but comfortably in a washcloth or small towel and lay her on your lap with her chest up. Hold her head securely with your thumb and index finger of one hand, and use the other to insert the syringe at about a 45-degree angle under the bird's chest feathers and into the muscle beneath.

You should remember to alternate the side you inject your bird on (say, left in the morning and right in the evening) to ensure that one side doesn't get overinjected and sore. Remain calm and talk to your bird in a soothing tone while you're administering the drugs. Before you both know it, the shot is over and your bird is one step closer to a complete recovery!

Topical Medication

This method, which is far less stressful than injections, provides medication directly to a part of a bird's body. Uses can include medications for eye infections, dry skin on the feet or legs, and sinus problems.

Parakeet Health Concerns

Although parakeets are generally hardy birds, they are prone to a few health problems, including scaly face, goiter, gout, obesity, and lipomas. They, like all birds, can also suffer from respiratory problems and other conditions that result from a vitamin A deficiency, especially if they eat diets that are high in seeds and low in vitamin-A-rich foods. Vitamin A deficiency can be prevented by feeding a varied, healthy diet.

Scaly Face

Scaly face is a condition caused by the knemidokoptes mite, a tiny relative of the spider that likes to burrow into the top layers of a parakeet's skin around

Mites can cause a relatively common condition called scaly face, which will leave white crusts on your bird's cere or the corners of her mouth. The condition is easy to treat—leaving your bird as healthy as beautiful as this one—but it can become serious if it's left untreated.

her cere, eyelids, vent, or legs. This burrowing leaves white crusts on the bird's cere or the corners of the mouth. If allowed to progress, scaly face can cause lesions on a bird's beak, eyelids, throat, vent, legs, and feet. Advanced cases can also cause beak deformation and horny appendages on a bird's face and legs. The leg appendages can interfere with a bird's ability to move her legs and toes.

If your avian veterinarian suspects your parakeet has scaly face, they will diagnose the condition by examining skin scrapings under a microscope. Although scaly face has the potential to be a serious condition, the good news is that it can be easily treated by a veterinarian using ivermectin, which will remove the mites and restore the skin to its normal appearance.

Although some over-the-counter remedies are sold to treat scaly face, a veterinarian-supervised course of treatment using ivermectin will clear up the problem more quickly and easily than using a nonprescription product.

Goiter

Goiter is an enlargement of the thyroid gland in a bird's throat. It is caused by an iodine deficiency and is most often seen in parakeets who eat seed-only diets.

Symptoms include difficulty breathing and swallowing, and regurgitation. Your veterinarian can determine if your parakeet has a goiter through X-rays and blood tests. Iodine supplements are used to treat the condition.

Gout

Gout is associated with kidney problems. Specifically, gouty birds have kidneys that are unable to remove excess nitrogen from the bird's bloodstream. This causes uric acid and urates to build up in the bird's body or in her joints. The exact cause of gout is unclear, but high levels of dietary sodium or calcium and inadequate fluid intake may contribute to the problem.

There are two forms of gout: articular gout, which affects a bird's lower leg joints as shiny, cream-colored swellings; and visceral gout, which affects a bird's internal organs and is difficult to diagnose. Articular gout, the type most often seen in parakeets, is a painful condition that causes an affected bird to go lame.

Currently there is no cure for gout. Treatment includes lowering protein levels and increasing the amount of fruits and vegetables in the bird's diet, along with treating any underlying infections that may affect kidney function. Veterinarians may be able to lower a bird's uric acid levels with medication, and they can also prescribe drugs to ease the bird's pain. Padded perches also seem to offer comfort to afflicted birds.

Regular exercise and time out of her cage will help keep your bird at a healthy weight.

Obesity

Obesity can sometimes be caused by a malfunctioning thyroid gland, but it is most often caused by a bird eating far more calories than she burns in a day. (English parakeets seem to be more prone to obesity than their American cousins.) To prevent this from happening to your pet parakeet, make sure she eats a well-balanced diet that is low in oil seeds and nuts (sunflower seeds, millet, peanuts, walnuts) and that she receives ample opportunity to exercise both in her cage and out of it during supervised "out times" on a playgym.

Lipoma

If your parakeet is overweight, you may notice that she has developed a fatty growth, or lipoma, that may impair her ability to fly. Some experts think these lipomas are linked to a lack of exercise in pet parakeets. The good news is that most lipomas can be removed safely by your veterinarian.

Bumblefoot

This is an infection of the sole of the bird's foot. It can cause redness and inflammation, swelling and lameness. Antibiotics, bandages, and surgery may be needed to treat the condition, which can be prevented by keeping a bird's cage clean and feeding her a well-balanced diet.

A parakeet spends all day on her feet, and foot conditions can be especially painful. A clean cage, a variety of perches, and a healthy diet will keep your bird safe from foot infections.

Giardia

This illness is caused by a protozoan called *Giardia psittaci*. This organism may cause a bird to have loose droppings, lose weight, pick her feathers, lose her appetite, and become depressed. Diagnosing this disease can be tricky, because the Giardia organism is difficult to detect in a bird's feces. The disease can be spread through contaminated food or water, and birds are not immune to reinfection once they've had it. Your veterinarian can recommend an appropriate medication to treat Giardia.

French Moult

This condition causes flight and tail feathers to develop improperly or not at all. Researchers believe the disease is caused by polyomavirus, which can be spread through contact with other birds, as well as from feather and fecal dust.

Adult birds can carry polyomavirus but not show any signs of the disease. These seemingly healthy birds can pass the virus to young birds who have never been exposed, and these young birds can die from polyomavirus rather quickly. Sick birds can become weak, lose their appetites, bleed beneath the skin, have enlarged abdomens, become paralyzed, regurgitate, and have diarrhea. Some birds with polyomavirus suddenly die.

At present, there is no cure, although a vaccine is under development. Protecting your pets against polyomavirus and other diseases is why it's important to quarantine new stock and to take precautions, including showering and changing clothes, before handling your pet when you've gone to other bird owners' homes, to bird marts that have large numbers of birds from different vendors on display, and to bird specialty stores with unhealthy stock.

Papilloma

Papillomas are benign tumors that can appear almost anywhere on a bird's skin, including her foot, leg, eyelid, or preen gland. These tumors, which are caused by a virus, can appear as small, crusty lesions, or they may be raised growths that have a bumpy texture or small projections. If a bird has a papilloma on her cloaca, the bird may appear to have a wet raspberry coming out of her vent.

Many papillomas can be left untreated without harm to the bird, but some must be removed by an avian veterinarian because a bird may pick at the growth and cause it to bleed.

Psittacine Beak and Feather Disease Syndrome

This virus has been a hot topic among birdkeepers since the late 1980s. It was first detected in cockatoos and was originally thought to be a cockatoo-specific problem. It has since been determined that more than forty species of parrots, including parakeets, can contract psittacine beak and feather disease syndrome (PBFDS), which causes a bird's feathers to become pinched or clubbed in appearance. Other symptoms include beak fractures and mouth ulcers. This highly contagious, fatal disease is most common in birds under three years of age, and there is no cure at present. A vaccine is under development at the University of Georgia.

Parakeet First Aid

Sometimes your pet will get herself into a situation that will require quick thinking and even quicker action on your part to help save her from serious injury or death. Here are some basic first-aid techniques that may prove useful in these situations. Before we get into the specific techniques, though, make sure you have your bird owner's first-aid kit. (See the box on page 91 for information on what to include.)

Here are some urgent medical situations that bird owners are likely to encounter, the reason that they are medical emergencies, the signs and symptoms your bird might show, and the recommended treatments for the problem.

Animal Bites

Infections can develop from bacteria on the biting animal's teeth and/or claws. Also, a bird's internal organs can be damaged by the bite. Sometimes the bite marks can be seen, but often the bird shows few, if any, signs of injury.

Call your veterinarian's office and transport the bird there immediately. Treatment for shock and antibiotics are often the courses of action veterinarians take to save birds who have been bitten.

Beak Injury

A bird needs both her upper and lower beak (also called the upper and lower mandible) to eat and preen properly.

An obvious symptom of an injury is when the bird is bleeding from her beak. This often occurs after the bird flies into a windowpane or mirror, or if she has a run-in with an operating ceiling fan. The beak may also be cracked or damaged, in which case portions of the beak may be missing. Infections can set in rather quickly if a beak is fractured or punctured.

Control bleeding (as described in the next section). Keep the bird calm and quiet. Contact your avian veterinarian's office.

Parrots use their beaks in almost as many ways as we use our hands (plus all the ways we use our mouths). Beak injuries are serious and need immediate medical attention.

Bleeding

A bird can only withstand about a 20 percent loss of blood volume (in a parakeet, that's only about twelve drops) and still recover from an injury. In the event of external bleeding, you will see blood on the bird, her cage, and/or her surroundings. In the case of internal bleeding, the bird may pass bloody droppings or bleed from her nares, mouth, or vent.

For external bleeding, apply direct pressure using a small piece of gauze or a cotton ball. If the bleeding doesn't stop with direct pressure, apply a coagulant, such as styptic powder (for nails and beaks only) or cornstarch (for broken feathers and skin injuries). If the bleeding stops, observe the bird to make sure the bleeding does not resume and the bird does not go into shock. Call your veterinarian's office if the bird seems weak or if she has lost a lot of blood, and arrange to take the bird in for further treatment.

In the case of broken blood feathers, you may have to remove the feather shaft to stop the bleeding. To do this, grasp the feather shaft as close to the skin as you can with a pair of needle-nosed pliers and pull out the shaft with a swift, steady motion. Apply direct pressure to the skin after you remove the feather shaft.

Breathing Problems

Respiratory problems in pet birds can be life threatening. The bird wheezes or clicks while breathing, bobs her tail, breathes with an open mouth, and has discharge from her nares or swelling around her eyes.

Keep the bird warm, place her in a bathroom with a hot shower running (but don't place her under the shower!) to help her breathe easier, and call your veterinarian's office.

Burns

Birds who are burned severely can go into shock and may die. A burned bird has reddened skin and burnt or greasy feathers. The bird may also show signs of shock (see page 93).

Mist the burned area with cool water. Lightly apply antibiotic cream or spray. Do not apply any oily or greasy substances, including butter. If the bird seems shocky or the burn is widespread, contact your veterinarian's office immediately for further instructions.

Concussion

A concussion results from a sharp blow to the head that can cause injury to the brain. Birds sometimes suffer concussions when they fly into mirrors or windows. They will seem stunned and may go into shock.

Keep the bird warm, prevent her from hurting herself further, and watch her carefully. Alert your veterinarian's office to the injury.

What to Do in an Emergency

If your bird requires urgent care, keep the following tips in mind:

Stay as calm as possible.
Stop any bleeding.
Keep the bird warm.
Keep the bird calm and quiet.
Call your veterinarian's office for additional instructions.
Describe to your vet what has happened to your bird.
Listen carefully to any instructions you receive.
Take your bird to the veterinarian's office or veterinary urgent care clinic as soon as possible.

Cloacal Prolapse

In this situation the bird's lower intestines, uterus, or cloaca protrudes from her vent. You will notice pink, red, brown, or black tissue protruding from her vent. Contact your veterinarian's office for immediate care. Your veterinarian can usually reposition the organs.

Egg Binding

Sometimes an egg blocks the hen's excretory system and makes it impossible for her to eliminate. Also, eggs can sometimes break inside the hen, which can lead to infection. An egg-bound hen strains to lay an egg unsuccessfully. She becomes fluffed and lethargic, sits on the floor of her cage, may be paralyzed, and may have a swollen abdomen.

Keep her warm, because this sometimes helps her pass the egg. Put her and her cage into a warm bathroom with a hot shower running to increase the humidity, which may also help her pass the egg. If your bird doesn't improve within a hour, contact your veterinarian.

Eye Injuries

Untreated eye problems may lead to blindness. Symptoms include swollen or pasty eyelids, discharge, cloudy eyeball, and increased rubbing of eye area. Examine the eye carefully for foreign bodies. Then contact your veterinarian for instructions.

Fractures

A fracture can cause a bird to go into shock. Depending on the type of fracture, infections can also set in. Birds most often break bones in their legs, so be on the lookout for a bird who is holding one leg at an odd angle or who isn't putting weight on one leg. Sudden swelling of a leg or wing, or a droopy wing, can also indicate fractures.

Confine the bird to her cage or a small carrier. Don't handle her unnecessarily. Keep her warm and contact your veterinarian.

Frostbite

A bird could lose toes or feet to frostbite. She could also go into shock and die as a result. You will see that the frostbitten area is very cold and dry to the touch and is pale in color. Warm up the damaged tissue gradually in a circulating bath of warm (not hot) water. Keep the bird warm and contact your veterinarian's office for further instructions.

Your Parakeet's First-Aid Kit

Assemble a bird owner's first-aid kit so that you will have some basic supplies on hand before your bird needs them. Here's what to include:

- Appropriate-size towels for catching and holding your bird
- Heating pad, heat lamp, or other heat source
- Styptic powder or cornstarch to stop bleeding (use styptic powder on beak and nails only)
- Blunt-tipped scissors
- Nail clippers and nail file
- Needle-nosed pliers to pull broken blood feathers
- Blunt-end tweezers
- Hydrogen peroxide or other disinfectant solution
- Eye irrigation solution
- Bandage materials such as gauze squares, masking tape (it doesn't stick to a bird's feathers as adhesive tape does) and gauze rolls
- Pedialyte or other energy supplement
- Eye dropper
- Penlight

Inhaled or Eaten Foreign Object

Birds can develop serious respiratory or digestive problems from foreign objects in their bodies. In the case of inhaled items, symptoms include wheezing and other respiratory problems. In the case of consumed objects, you may have seen the bird playing with a small item that suddenly cannot be found.

If you suspect that your bird has inhaled or eaten something she shouldn't, contact your veterinarian's office immediately.

Lead Poisoning

Birds can die from lead poisoning. A bird with lead poisoning may act depressed or weak. She may be blind, or she may walk in circles at the bottom of her cage. She may regurgitate or pass droppings that resemble tomato juice.

Contact your avian veterinarian immediately. Lead poisoning requires a quick start to treatment, and the treatment may require several days or weeks to complete successfully.

Overheating

High body temperatures can kill a bird. An overheated bird will try to make herself thin. She will hold her wings away from her body, open her mouth, and roll her tongue in an attempt to cool herself. Birds don't have sweat glands, so they must try to cool their bodies by exposing as much of their skin's surface as they can to moving air.

Cool the bird off by putting her in front of a fan (make sure the blades are screened so the bird doesn't injure herself further), by spraying her with cool water, or by having her stand in a bowl of cool water. Let the bird drink cool water if she can (if she can't, offer her cool water with an eyedropper) and contact your veterinarian.

Very old bird cages or fancy cages that have been imported from some countries may contain lead in the bars. Buy a new cage to be sure your bird is safe from lead poisoning.

Poisoning

Poisons can kill a small bird quickly. Poisoned birds may suddenly regurgitate, have diarrhea or bloody droppings, and have redness or burns around their mouths. They may also go into convulsions, become paralyzed, or go into shock. Put the poison out of your bird's reach. Contact your veterinarian for further instructions. Be prepared to take the poison with you to the vet's office in case they need to contact a poison control center for further information.

Birds will chew on anything they can get their beaks on. Protect your bird from poisoning by putting harmful items out of her reach.

Seizures

Seizures can indicate a number of serious conditions, including lead poisoning, infections, nutritional deficiency, heat stroke, and epilepsy. The bird goes into a seizure that lasts from a few seconds to a minute. Afterward, she seems dazed and may stay on the cage floor for several hours. She may also appear unsteady and not perch.

Keep the bird from hurting herself by removing everything you can from her cage. Cover the bird's cage with a towel and darken the room to reduce the bird's stress level. Contact your veterinarian's office immediately for further instructions.

Shock

Shock occurs when the bird's circulatory system cannot move the blood supply around the bird's body. This is a serious condition that can lead to death if left untreated. Shocky birds may act depressed, they may breathe rapidly, and they may have a fluffed appearance. If your bird displays these signs in conjunction with a recent accident, suspect shock and take appropriate action.

Keep your bird warm, cover her cage, and transport her to your veterinarian's office as soon as possible.

Can You Catch Avian Flu from Your Bird?

Zoonotic diseases, or diseases that can be passed between animals and people, have gotten a great deal of attention in the first part of the twenty-first century, thanks to diseases such as avian flu, which came to public attention in late 2003 when outbreaks were reported in Asia. Ten countries reported outbreaks in 2004, and fifty-five people worldwide contracted the disease from birds. When this book went to press, the Centers for Disease Control and Prevention had a plan in place to combat avian flu in the event of an outbreak in the United States, and vaccines to combat the disease are under development.

Avian flu is an infectious disease that is caused by Type A strains of the influenza virus. It infects mostly waterfowl, such as ducks, and it can spread to domestic poultry. Wild birds worldwide may be carriers of avian flu. Carrier birds often do not show signs of illness, but they shed the virus through their droppings, nasal secretions, or saliva.

Avian flu is of particular concern to poultry farmers in the United States. Since 1997, about sixteen outbreaks of avian flu have been reported on U.S. poultry farms. These outbreaks were classified as low pathogenic, which means few birds became ill or died. This is in direct contrast to the cases reported in Asia in 2003 and 2004, when thousands of birds became ill or were euthanized to stop the spread of the disease.

People can catch avian flu by coming in contact with the droppings of infected birds or with the birds themselves. This is what happened in Asia during the outbreaks in 2003 and 2004. Symptoms of avian flu in people can range from the typical flu-like symptoms, such as fever, cough, sore throat, and muscle aches, to eye infection, pneumonia, and other life-threatening complications. Clinical signs in birds can vary, from birds who show no signs of illness to any of the following: lack of energy and appetite, decreased egg production, soft-shelled or misshapen eggs, nasal discharge, sneezing, a lack of coordination, and loose droppings.

Let me emphasize that it is extremely unlikely that your parakeet is a carrier of avian flu or that you could catch avian flu from your pet. Avian flu is a greater concern for poultry farmers and bird breeders than it is for the average pet bird owner. I am including information here because the topic has received attention in television and newspaper reports.

Caring for Older Birds

Although older parakeets are far from being delicate hothouse flowers, owners of these birds should pay more attention to their pets' diets to ensure the bird continues to receive a varied diet that is low in fat. Also pay special attention to the temperature of the room in which the bird is kept during cool weather. Add supplemental heat by using an incandescent lightbulb covered with a reflector on one end of your bird's cage. This enables the bird to move closer to the heat source if she is cold and away from it if she becomes too warm. Make sure the bulb is far enough away from the cage so that your pet cannot burn herself on the reflector or the bulb.

As your parakeet ages, the need to watch her daily routine becomes even more important, since health problems that are caught early are easier to treat. Older pet birds are prone to a number of health problems, including tumors, vision problems, thyroid gland insufficiencies, chlamydiosis, and upper respiratory infections.

Tumors

Parakeets can develop tumors as early as age five, although if a bird passes the age of seven without developing a tumor, she will probably live out her life tumor free. If you notice that your pet's breastbone sticks out a little more than it used to or that your bird has difficulty perching, schedule an evaluation with your avian veterinarian; both of these signs indicate possible tumors. Tumors develop in pet birds most frequently in the nerves off the bird's spine. A tumor in this spot can impair kidney and gonad function, which can put pressure on the nerve that runs into the bird's leg.

Vision Problems

Vision problems can show themselves in several ways. Your pet may no longer be able to judge distances well, or her eyes may appear clouded over. Just as in older people, cataracts can appear in older parakeets.

Thyroid Problems

Thyroid problems occur frequently in older parrots, but they aren't discussed often. These problems manifest in two main ways: a deficiency in the bird's hormonal system or a need for supplemental iodine in the diet. If your parakeet suddenly gains weight and develops fat deposits that resemble tumors, contact your avian veterinarian to have her examined.

Don't let the loss of one beloved parakeet keep you from owning other birds.

Although they may not seem to be connected, a thyroid problem may show itself in a longer-than-average molt. If you notice that your parakeet's molting period seems unusually long as she ages, talk to your avian veterinarian. A hormonal supplement may be required to help keep your bird healthy.

When Your Parakeet Dies

Although birds are relatively long-lived pets, eventually the wonderful relationship between bird and owner ends when the bird dies. While no one has an easy time accepting the death of a beloved pet, children may have more difficulty with the loss than adults.

Let your child know that it's okay to feel sad about losing your parakeet. Encourage your child to draw pictures of the bird, to make a collage using photos of your pet parakeet or pictures of parakeets from magazines, to write stories or poems about her, and to talk about the loss. Also explain to the child that these sad feelings will pass with time.

Regardless of a child's age, being honest about the loss of your parakeet is the best approach to help all family members cope with the loss.

While helping their children cope with the death of a pet, parents need to remember that it's okay for adults to feel sad, too. Don't diminish your feelings of loss by saying, "It's only a bird." Pets fill important roles in our lives and our families. Whenever we lose someone close to us, we grieve. If someone in your family needs to discuss the loss further, pet grief counselors are available to help. Veterinary schools, state and regional veterinary associations, and humane societies around the United States offer such services to grieving pet owners. (You'll find a list of them in the appendix.) Your avian veterinarian's office may know of pet loss support groups in your area, or you may be able to find one online.

Although you may feel as though you never want another bird because of the pain caused by your parakeet's death, don't let the loss of your parakeet keep you from owning other

Pets fill important roles in our lives, and losing one is always difficult.

birds. While you can never replace an individual parakeet, you may find that you miss having a feathered companion around your house. Some people will want a new pet bird almost immediately after suffering a loss, while others will want to wait a few weeks or months before bringing another bird home. Maybe you want another parakeet, or perhaps you'd like to try owning a different avian species. Discuss bringing home a new pet bird with your family, your avian veterinarian, and bird breeders in your area. Together, I'm sure you can work out a plan that's best for you.

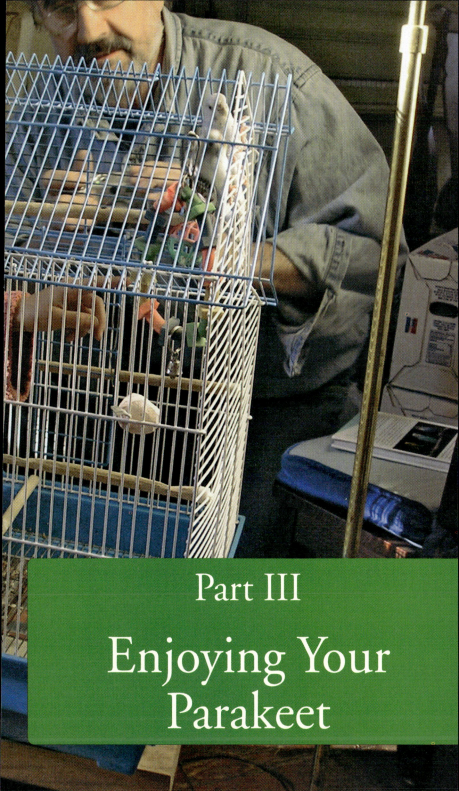

Part III

Enjoying Your Parakeet

Chapter 9

Parakeet Behavior

As a new bird owner, you're probably wondering what constitutes normal behavior for your pet and what behaviors indicate that something isn't quite right with your parakeet.

In this chapter I'll list common normal parrot behaviors. Use them as a starting point to determine what behaviors are normal for your pet bird. Compare them against the behaviors listed at the end of the chapter, which often indicate illness. If your bird shows any signs of illness, make an appointment with your avian veterinarian for an immediate evaluation. Birds are experts at hiding signs of illness, so by the time a bird looks or acts sick, he is really seriously ill.

As you get to know your pet and as he settles into his new routine in your home, you'll soon learn exactly what behaviors are normal for your pet. It's important for you as a bird owner to learn what is normal for your parakeet, because your avian veterinarian will often ask for your observations during routine examinations as well as during times of illness.

Common Parakeet Behaviors

The following common parakeet behaviors will help you better understand your new feathered friend!

Beak Grinding

If you hear your bird making odd little grinding noises as he's drifting off to sleep, don't be alarmed! Beak grinding is a sign of a contented parakeet and it's commonly heard as a bird settles in for the night.

Beak Wiping

After a meal it's common for a parakeet to wipe his beak against a perch or on the cage floor to clean it. If something particularly persistent is stuck to a parakeet's beak, he will use his foot to clean his beak.

Birdie Aerobics

This is how I describe a sudden bout of stretching that all parrots seem prone to. An otherwise calm bird will suddenly grab the cage bars and stretch the wing and leg muscles on one side of his body, or he will raise both wings high.

Eye Pinning

This is what happens when your parakeet sees something that excites him. His pupils will become large, then contract, then get large again. Birds will pin their eyes when they see a favorite food, a favored person, another bird, or a special toy. In larger parrots, this can also be a sign of confused emotions that can leave an owner vulnerable to a nasty bite. Your parakeet may also bite when he's in "emotional overload," so watch out!

Feather Picking

Don't confuse this with preening (see more on preening later in this section). Feather picking results from physiological problems, such as a dietary imbalance, a hormonal change, a thyroid problem, or an infection of the skin or feathers. It can also be caused by an emotional upset, such as a change in the owner's appearance, a change in the bird's routine, another pet being added to the home, a new baby in the home, or a number of other factors. Although it looks painful to us, some birds seem to find the routine of pulling out their feathers emotionally soothing.

When a bird is excited, his pupils become large, then contract, then get large again. The behavior is called pinning.

Once feather picking begins, it may be difficult to get a bird to stop. The good news is that parakeets are not as prone to this condition as other larger parrots are. If you keep more than one parakeet, however, be aware that they sometimes pick out each other's feathers. If this occurs, you may have to house your birds in separate cages to allow the plucked bird to regrow his plumage.

Fluffing

This is often a prelude to preening or a tension releaser. If your bird fluffs up, stays fluffed, and resembles a little feathered pinecone, however, contact your avian veterinarian for an appointment, because fluffed feathers can be an indicator of illness.

Jealousy

Some parakeets become very possessive of their owners and these jealous birds demonstrate their displeasure in a number of ways. This can include tearing up their cages, nibbling on their owners' hands, or screaming, which, while not as annoying as the noise made by a cockatoo or macaw, can nonetheless diminish your enjoyment of your parakeet.

A little fluffing may just be your bird's way of easing his stress.

To prevent your parakeet from becoming a problem pet, be sure to give him the opportunity to entertain himself in his cage alone from time to time. Don't reward his screaming for attention (you'll soon learn which screams are just for the joy of making noise and which ones indicate a pet is in danger or pain), and don't bribe your pet into silence with treats while you are out of the room or on the phone. If you do, your bird will soon have you wrapped around his wing feathers and will take full advantage of the situation.

Mutual Preening

This is part of the preening behavior described on the next page. It can take place between birds or between birds and their owners. It is a sign of

Feathered Warnings

Your bird's feathers are one of the most fascinating organs of his body. The bird uses feathers for movement, warmth, and balance, among other things. The following are some feather-related behaviors that can indicate health problems.

Fluffing: A healthy parakeet will fluff before preening or for short periods. If your parakeet seems to remain fluffed up for an extended period, see your avian veterinarian. This can be a sign of illness.

Mutual preening: Two birds will preen each other affectionately, but if you notice excessive feather loss, make sure one bird is not picking on the other and pulling out healthy feathers.

Feather picking: A healthy bird will preen often to keep his feathers in top shape. However, a bird under stress may start to preen excessively and severe feather loss can result.

affection reserved for best friends or mates, so consider it an honor if your parakeet wants to preen your eyebrows, hair, mustache or beard, or your arms and hands.

Pair Bonding

Mated pairs bond, but so do best bird buddies of the same sex. Buddy pairs will demonstrate some of the same behavior as mated pairs, including sitting close to each other, preening each other, and mimicking one another's actions, such as stretching or scratching, often at the same time.

Preening

This is part of a parakeet's normal routine. You will see your bird ruffling and straightening his feathers each day. He will also take oil from the uropygial or preen gland at the base of his tail and put the oil on the rest of his feathers, so don't be concerned if you see your pet seeming to peck or bite at his tail. If, during molting, your bird seems to remove whole feathers, don't panic! Old, worn feathers are pushed out by incoming new ones, which makes the old feathers loose and easy to remove.

Regurgitating

If you see that your bird is pinning his eyes, bobbing his head, and pumping his neck and crop muscles, he is about to regurgitate some food for you. Birds regurgitate for their mates during breeding season and for their young while raising chicks. It is a mark of great affection to have your bird regurgitate his dinner for you, so try not to be too disgusted if your pet starts bringing up his last meal.

Resting on One Foot

Do not be alarmed if you see your parakeet occasionally resting on only one foot. This is normal behavior (the other foot is often drawn up into the belly feathers). If your bird is always using both feet to perch, please contact your avian veterinarian because this can indicate a health problem.

Side-Stepping

This is a common movement when a parakeet is working his way across his cage on a perch. Other common movements include climbing and flying (if the cage is large enough).

Birds like to preen their best friends. That may be another bird, or it may be you.

Scratching

Parakeets have remarkably flexible leg joints, which they sometimes use to bring their legs up and behind their wings to scratch their heads. Parakeets may be the only psittacine birds who do this; larger parrots bring their heads and feet together in front of their bodies to scratch.

Vocalization

Many parrots vocalize around sunrise and sunset, which I believe hearkens back to wild flock behavior in which parrots call to each other to start and end their days. Parakeets in the wild do this too,

Birds form bonds with their mates and with their best buddies.

especially at day's end when they chirp softly as they ready themselves for sleep. You may also notice if you keep more than one parakeet that the birds will call to each other during the day if they are in separate rooms (perhaps one is on a playgym in the family room while the other is in his cage in the dining room). These contact calls help birds keep track of each other, both in the wild and in your home.

If something startles your parakeet, you may hear him make a short, shrill call to signal that something has alarmed him. Parakeets can also express their pleasure or displeasure through vocalization. Soft chirps indicate a happy bird, while shrieks indicate that something is amiss in your bird's world.

Stress

This can show itself in many ways in your bird's behavior, including shaking, diarrhea, rapid breathing, wing and tail fanning, screaming, feather picking, poor sleeping habits, and loss of appetite. Over a period of time, stress can harm your parakeet's health.

To prevent your bird from becoming stressed, try to provide him with as normal and regular a routine as possible. Parrots are, for the most part, creatures of habit, and they don't always adapt well to sudden changes in their environment

Abnormal Behaviors

If your parakeet shows signs of any of the following behaviors, make an appointment with your avian veterinarian because they can indicate illness in a pet bird:

- Sleeping too much
- Sitting with feathers fluffed for long periods of time, even on warm days
- Listlessness
- Lack of appetite
- Regurgitating whole seeds
- Loss of balance or inability to perch
- Feather picking
- Feather chewing

or schedule. If you do have to change something, talk to your parrot about it first. I know it seems crazy, but telling your bird what you're going to do before you do it may actually help reduce his stress. I received this advice from avian behaviorist Christine Davis, and now I explain what I'm doing every time I rearrange the living room or leave my bird at the vet's office for boarding during business trips. If you're going to be away on vacation, tell your bird how long you'll be gone and count the days out on your fingers in front of the bird or show him a calendar.

Chapter 10

Having Fun with Your Parakeet

Now that you've learned the basics of caring for your new parakeet, it's time to really enjoy your pet's companionship. Try to spend time with your bird each day to make sure her emotional needs for companionship are met. Remember that you and your family are substituting for your parakeet's flock and that your parakeet is a very social little bird who needs companionship regularly to feel secure and content in her surroundings.

To spend time with your pet each day, it's best to train her to follow simple commands that make her easier to handle. This way, you can take your parakeet with you while you are doing homework, talking on the phone, or watching television. Your bird will benefit from the time spent with you in a different environment than her cage, and you will have more time to enjoy your pet. Whenever your pet is out of her cage, be sure to supervise her carefully to ensure she stays safe and healthy! (Chapter 4 has plenty of advice on how to make your home safe for your bird.)

Taming Your Parakeet

Taming a parrot was one of the most popular topics of discussion when I worked at *Bird Talk,* and the discussion continues today among avian behaviorists and their clients, in bird club meetings, books and magazine articles, and on the Internet. The bottom line, though, is that taming and training a parakeet (or any bird) takes a great deal of time and patience on the part of the bird owner. You must first gain your pet's trust, and then you must work to never lose it.

When your parakeet has settled into her new home, start getting to know her by simply placing your hand in her cage.

A good first step in taming your parakeet is getting her to feel comfortable around you. To do this, give your bird a bit of warning before you approach her cage. Don't sneak up on your bird and try not to startle her. Call her name when you walk into the room. Try to be quiet and move slowly around your pet, because these gestures will help her become more comfortable with you. Keep your hands behind you and reassure the bird that you aren't there to harm her, that everything is all right, and that she's a wonderful pet.

After your bird is comfortable having you in the same room, you may want to try placing your hand in her cage as a first step toward taking her out. Place your hand in your bird's cage and hold it there for a few seconds. Don't be surprised if your bird flutters around and squawks at first at the "intruder."

Continue this process daily, leaving your hand in the cage for slightly longer periods each day. Within a few days, your parakeet won't make a fuss about your hand being in her space, and she may even come over to investigate this new perch. Do not remove your hand from the cage the first time your parakeet lands on it; just let the bird become accustomed to perching on your hand.

After several successful perching attempts on successive days, try to take your hand out of the cage with your bird on it. Some parakeets will take to this new adventure willingly, while others are reluctant to leave the safety and security of home. (Be sure your bird's wings are clipped and all doors and windows in your home are secured before taking your bird out of her cage.)

Other Approaches

If your bird doesn't seem to respond to this method, you can try an alternate taming method. Take the bird out of her cage and into a small room, such as a bathroom, that has been bird-proofed (that is, the toilet lid is down, the shower door is closed, and the bathroom hasn't been cleaned recently with any cleansers that have strong chemical odors). Sit down on the floor, place your bird in front of you, and begin playing with the bird. Don't be surprised if your bird tries to fly a few times. With clipped wings, however, she won't get very far and will give up trying after a few failed attempts.

Breeder Charlene Beane has demonstrated her parakeet taming method for me several times, and its simplicity and effectiveness always amaze me. Charlene will hold a bird who isn't quite tame close to her chest so the bird can hear her heartbeat, which seems to calm the bird. She then talks to the bird in a low, soothing tone and explains that the bird will make someone a wonderful pet. As she does this, she gently begins to stroke the parakeet's back, which helps the bird relax. She continues to explain the bird's role as a perfect pet for about five minutes, stroking the bird as she talks. Pretty soon, the bird is calm and ready to be handled.

Step Up, Step Down

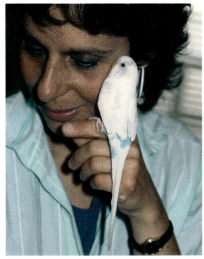

Once you've calmed your parakeet using Charlene's method, see if you can make perching on your hand a game for your pet. Once she masters perching on your hand, you can teach her to step up by gently pressing your finger up and into the bird's belly. This will cause the bird to step up. As she does so, say "step up" or "up." Before long, your bird will respond to this command without much prompting.

Along with the up command, you may want to teach your parakeet the down command. When you put the bird down on her cage

The first thing to teach your bird is to step up into your hand, then down onto a perch or playgym.

or playgym, simply say "down" as she steps off your hand. These two simple commands give you a great deal of control over your bird, because you can say "up" to put an unruly bird back in her cage and you can say "down" to a parrot who needs to go to bed as you put her in her cage at night.

After your bird has mastered the up and down commands, encourage her to climb a "ladder" by moving her from index finger to index finger (the "rungs"). Keep taming sessions short (about ten minutes is the maximum parakeet attention span) and make it fun so taming is enjoyable for both of you.

Petting

After your bird has become comfortable sitting on your hand, try petting her. Birds seem to like to have their heads, backs, cheek patches, under wing areas, and eye areas (including the closed eyelids) scratched or petted lightly. Quite a few like to have a spot low on their back at the base of their tail (over their preen glands) rubbed. Many birds do not enjoy having their stomachs scratched, although yours may think this is heaven! You'll have to experiment to see where your bird likes to be petted. You'll know you're successful if your bird clicks or grinds her beak, pins her eyes, or settles onto your hand or your lap with a completely relaxed, blissful expression on her face.

Many parakeets like having their heads, backs, cheek patches, under wing areas, and eye areas scratched or petted lightly.

Some people may try to tell you that you need to wear gloves while taming your parakeet to protect yourself from a bite. I recommend against this. A parakeet generally doesn't bite *that* hard and wearing gloves will only make your hands appear more scary to your bird. If your pet is scared, taming her will take more time and patience on your part, which may make the process less enjoyable for you both.

Toilet Training

Although some people don't believe it, parakeets and other parrots can be toilet trained so they don't eliminate on their owners. If you want to toilet train your bird, you will have to choose a word or phrase that will mean the act of eliminating to your pet, such as "poop" or "go potty." While you're training your pet to associate the word or phrase with the action, you will have to train yourself to recognize what body language and actions indicate your parakeet is about to eliminate, such as shifting around or squatting slightly. Use the phrase every time you see your parakeet eliminate.

Once your bird seems to associate "go potty" with eliminating, you can try picking her up and holding her until she starts to shift or squat. Tell the bird to "go potty" while placing her on her cage, where she can eliminate. Once she's done, pick your bird up again and praise her for being such a smart bird!

Expect a few accidents while you are both learning this trick, but soon you'll have a toilet-trained bird: You can put her on her cage about every twenty minutes or so, give her the command, and expect the bird to eliminate on command.

Naughty Parakeets

To maintain the bind of trust you have built with your bird through taming, you must be careful not to lose your temper with your bird and

Birds will be birds. Sometimes yours will need a little time alone to calm down.

never hit her. Birds are very sensitive, intelligent creatures who do not deserve to be hit, no matter how you may feel in a moment of anger.

Although parrots are clever creatures, they are not linear cause-and-effect thinkers. If a parrot commits action A (chewing on some molding under your kitchen cabinets, for example), she won't associate reaction B (you yelling at her, locking her in her cage, or otherwise punishing her) with the original misbehavior. As a result, most traditional forms of discipline are ineffective with parrots.

So what do you do when your parakeet misbehaves? Try to catch her in the act. Look at your bird sternly and tell her "no" in a firm voice. If the bird is climbing on or chewing something she shouldn't, remove her from the source of danger and temptation as you tell her "no."

If your bird has wound herself up into a screaming fit, sometimes a little time out in her cage (between five and ten minutes in most cases) with the cover on does wonders to calm her down. Once the screaming stops and the bird calms down enough to play quietly, eat, or simply move around her cage, the cover comes off to reveal a well-behaved, calm pet.

Will My Parakeet Talk?

One of the most appealing aspects of parakeet ownership is this species' reputation as talented talkers. Although many parakeets learn to talk, none of them is guaranteed to talk. The tips here will help you teach your parakeet to talk, but please don't be disappointed if your bird never utters a word.

Remember that language, whether it's parakeet or human, helps members of a species or group communicate. Most baby birds learn the language of their parents because it helps them communicate within their family and their flock. A pet parakeet raised with people may learn to imitate the sounds she hears her human family make, but if you have more than one parakeet the birds may find communicating with each other easier and more enjoyable than trying to learn your language.

Although most parakeets raised around humans do learn to talk, some choose to make other sounds. Calvin, a physically challenged bird I used to bird-sit, had ample opportunity to learn human speech from his owner and other people who saw him regularly. Instead of speaking, though, Calvin chose to imitate the computer printer, modem, and other machines found in his owner's office.

Most experts say the best time to teach a parakeet to talk is between the time she leaves the nest and her first birthday. If you have an adult parakeet, the chances of her learning to talk are less than if you start with a young bird. Male birds may be more likely to talk, but I have heard of some talkative females, too.

Talking Tips

You will be more successful in training a parakeet to talk if you keep a single pet bird, rather than a pair. Birds kept in pairs or groups are more likely to bond with other birds than with people. By the same token, don't give your bird any toys with mirrors on them if you want the bird to learn to talk, since your bird will think the bird in the mirror is a potential cagemate with whom she can bond.

Start with a young bird, because the younger the bird is, the more likely she is to want to mimic human speech.

Pick one phrase to start with. Keep it short and simple, such as the bird's name. Say the phrase slowly so the bird learns it clearly. Some people teach their parakeets to talk by rattling off words and phrases quickly, only to be disappointed when the bird repeats them in a blurred jumble that cannot be understood.

Be sure to say the chosen phrase with emphasis and enthusiasm. Birds like drama and seem to learn words that are said emphatically—which may be why some of them pick up bad language so quickly!

Try to use phrases that make sense in context. For instance, say "good morning" or "hello" when you uncover the bird's cage each day. Say "good-bye" when you leave the room, or ask "want a treat?" when you offer your parakeet her meals. Phrases that make sense are also more likely to be used by you and other members of your family when conversing with your bird. The more your bird hears an interesting word or phrase, the more likely she is to say that phrase some day.

The company of other birds, or her own lovely image in a mirror, make your bird less likely to talk. However, don't let your bird get lonely or bored just to boost the chances that she'll talk. Your parakeet may never speak, but she will always be your fabulous pet.

Don't change the phrase around. If you're teaching your bird to say "hello," for example, don't say "hello" one day, then "hi" the next, followed by "hi, Petey!" (or whatever your bird's name is) another day.

Keep training sessions short. Parakeet breeders recommend ten- to fifteen-minute sessions.

Train your bird in a quiet area. Think of how distracting it is when someone is trying to talk to you with a radio or television blaring in the background. It's hard to hear what the other person is saying under those conditions, isn't it? Your parakeet won't be able to hear you any better or understand what you are trying to accomplish if you try to train her in the midst of noisy distractions. Be sure to keep your parakeet involved in your family's routine, though, because isolating her completely won't help her feel comfortable and part of the family. Remember that a bird needs to feel comfortable in her environment before she will draw attention to herself by talking.

Be patient with your pet. Stop the sessions if you find you are getting frustrated. Your parakeet will sense that something is bothering you and will react by becoming bothered herself. This is not an ideal situation for you or your bird. Try to keep your mood upbeat. Smile a lot and praise your pet when she does well!

Most birds never learn to talk, but they are always fascinating. Just love your pets and look to them for friendship; they won't disappoint you.

Talking Success Stories

Although parakeets aren't guaranteed to talk, Puck, a parakeet in northern California, holds the Guinness World Record for having the largest vocabulary of any animal. Puck's owner estimates that her bird has a 1,728-word vocabulary!

Sparkie, a parakeet who lived in Great Britain from 1954 to 1962, held the record for a talking bird in his time. He won the BBC's Cage Word Contest in 1958 by reciting eight four-line nursery rhymes without stopping. At the time of his death, Sparkie had a vocabulary of 531 words and 383 sentences.

Graduate to more difficult phrases as your bird masters simple words. Consider keeping a log of the words your bird knows. (This is especially helpful if more than one person will be working with the parakeet.)

When you aren't talking to your parakeet, try listening to her. Parakeets and other birds sometimes mumble to themselves to practice talking as they drift off to sleep. Because a parakeet has a very small voice, you'll have to listen carefully to hear if your pet is making progress.

You're probably wondering if the talking tapes and CDs sold in pet supply stores and through advertisements in bird magazines work. The most realistic answer I can give is "sometimes." Some birds learn from the repetition of the tapes and CDs that, fortunately, have gotten livelier and more interesting in recent years. Other birds benefit from having their owners make tapes of the phrases the bird is currently learning and hearing those tapes when their owners aren't around. I recommend against playing a constant barrage of taped phrases during the day, because the bird is likely to get bored hearing the same thing for hours on end. If she's bored, the bird will be more likely to tune out the tape and the training.

Finally, if your patient, consistent training seems to be going nowhere, you may have to accept the fact that your parakeet isn't going to talk. We finally had to do this with my parakeet, Charlie. Despite my mother's most patient attempts to teach the bird to say "pretty bird," he never learned to talk. My mother did things by the book, too. She spoke in a bright, cheerful voice, she kept the training sessions short, she kept a positive attitude and tone when talking to the bird, and she displayed patience that rivaled Job's. But Charlie remained silent. Perhaps he was too old, perhaps he was too isolated, or perhaps he just wasn't interested in the phrase.

As I've said before, don't be too disappointed if your pet doesn't learn to talk. Most birds don't, and talking ability should never be the primary reason for owning a bird. If you end up with a pet who doesn't talk, continue to love her for the unique creature she is.

Tricks to Teach Your Parakeet

One of the best ways to spend time with your parakeet is to teach her to do simple tricks. Your bird will come to expect and enjoy the extra attention you give her during training sessions, and you will see a stronger bond develop between you and your bird as the training progresses.

Before you begin to teach your parakeet tricks, make sure you have the patience and perseverance to undertake training sessions. Birds sometimes behave as we expect them to, but sometimes they want to do what they want to do, and it's up to you not to become frustrated or angry with your pet when she does not behave as you expect. Anger and frustration can damage the relationship you have with your bird, so be sure to be patient and cheerful during each training session.

As you begin to plan what tricks you will teach your parakeet, notice what your bird likes to do and make it part of her trick training. You will soon find it's much easier to expand on one or more of your bird's natural behaviors, and that will make trick training easier and more enjoyable for both of you. For example, some parakeets like to climb while others may enjoy holding their wings in the air and stretching (this can be turned into an eagle pose without too much effort). Still others amuse themselves by using their beaks to examine a wide variety of items in their environment, and you can teach them to touch objects as you name them.

My stepdaughter Rhonda is quite an accomplished parakeet trainer. She received her parakeet, Andre, as a gift from her father when she was nine. She began working with him daily after school and soon had him doing all sorts of tricks, including responding to his name and to the "stop" command, giving kisses, and talking on the telephone.

One of Andre's better tricks was the coin drop. Rhonda taught him to pick a coin up from the table and drop it in front of whomever she designated. Andre quickly took this trick in a different direction: He would run to the edge of the table with the coin and drop it, which meant Rhonda had to bend over and pick it up. Andre seemed to enjoy "teaching" Rhonda to do this as much as she enjoyed teaching him tricks.

But the best trick Andre learned was something that could be described as the crosswalk trick. Because Andre was allowed out of his cage at various times during the day, Rhonda worried that someone might step on her little bird, so she taught him to look both ways whenever he came out of her room into the hall and to stop and wait for people to pass him before he proceeded.

Because Rhonda worked with Andre every day, he became accustomed to the training sessions. They became part of her daily interaction with her pet, and she provided positive reinforcement with cuddles and verbal praise (as well as occasional treats) to reward Andre when he behaved as she wanted. She rarely lost patience with her bird, and she talked to him in a sweet, positive tone. She also played with him and cared for him, and over time a strong bond developed between them. I believe he really wanted to please her, which was part of the reason she was so successful at teaching him to do tricks.

Tips for Better Training

To make the most of your parakeet training sessions, keep the following points in mind.

Know what your bird likes and dislikes. If your bird is naturally playful, she will be a better candidate to learn tricks than a bird who is content to sit on her owner's hand for head scratching.

Provide several short training sessions each day. Pet birds have short attention spans, and they tend to become cranky if you try to teach them something once you've exceeded that attention span. Ten minutes or less, several times a day, is usually more effective than one longer session.

Make the sessions fun. Remember that these training sessions are supposed to be enjoyable for both you and your bird, and immediately end any session that is not going well.

Reward your bird's good behavior with a combination of food treats, verbal praise, petting, or cuddling. If your bird loves to have her head nape scratched, for instance, give this area extra attention when your bird performs her trick correctly. This way she will learn to respond to different types of rewards, rather than just waiting for a favorite food treat to come her way.

Choose tricks to teach your bird that make use of things she already likes to do.

Appreciate your bird for the unique individual she is. Love your bird because she is your pet, not because of the tricks she can do. Some birds are natural show-offs, while others are more reserved. If you have a quick trick learner, teach the bird tricks and add to her repertoire over time. If your bird doesn't seem to enjoy learning tricks, don't force the issue. Appreciate your bird for her other wonderful qualities and love her as your pet.

Your parakeet is a bright bird and can learn to perform a wide variety of tricks. Her repertoire of learned behaviors is limited only by your imagination and your patience during the training process. Listed here are some beginning tricks to teach your pet. As your training skills improve, you will undoubtedly come up with some tricks that are unique to you and your bird. Good luck, and remember to have fun!

Nod Your Head

A parakeet who interacts well with her owner and is unafraid of showing off for strangers is a good candidate to learn to nod her head yes and shake her head no.

To teach your bird to nod her head, hold a small portion of her favorite treat just out of reach of her beak and slowly bob it up and down. Your parakeet will nod her head as she follows the motion of the treat, trying to catch it with her beak. Give her verbal praise, such as "is that a yes?" as she nods, so she will associate the words with the motion.

Practice this trick with the treat and the verbal praise, and gradually increase the praise while eliminating the treat.

To teach your parakeet to shake her head no, repeat the steps above but move the treat side to side instead of up and down, so your bird's head will shake side to side to indicate no. Provide different verbal praise, such as "is that a no?" as you move the treat from side to side.

Pose Like an Eagle

A parakeet who enjoys being petted under her wings is a very good candidate to learn to pose like an eagle. Birds who do not enjoy being petted under their wings can also learn this trick, but training them may take a little longer.

Start your training by gently tickling your parakeet under each wing tip with your index finger. This will cause your parakeet to raise her wings. Praise her at this point by saying something like "good eagle, good bird" so your parakeet will begin to associate the word "eagle" with raising her wings.

Practice the combination of gentle tickling and verbal praise at each training session. Increase the use of verbal praise and decrease the tickling until your parakeet responds to your words alone.

Play Dead

A parakeet who enjoys being petted and is willing to be turned over by her owner is a good candidate for learning to play dead. First, you must get your bird accustomed to the feel of your hand on her back as she

Birds in the parrot family are among the smartest of all companion animals and can learn a large repertoire of behaviors. But all learning is built upon a base of friendship and trust between you and your parakeet.

perches on her cage or playgym. When the bird seems comfortable with your hand on her back, hold her between your hands on her side.

After your parakeet is used to being held on her side between your hands, move to holding her on her back between your hands. Once she seems content to lie this way, remove the hand you have on your bird's feet or belly, and you have a bird playing dead in your hand!

A friend of mine trained her cockatoo to go to sleep in this way, and he enjoys showing off his trick to her friends. She flips the bird over in her hands, tells him, "night-night," and he responds with a "night-night" of his own. He closes his eyes and she carries him to his cage, where he climbs onto his sleeping perch for the night. She is the only person in her family the bird allows to do this trick—he doesn't seem to think anyone else can get it right!

Your bird must have to have an incredible amount of trust in you before she will allow you to flip her over onto her back. Lying on her back is not a normal parrot posture. If your parakeet seems distressed when you flip her onto her back, teach her another trick instead of causing her undue stress by insisting she learn this one.

Learning More About Your Parakeet

Books

Alderton, David, *Birdkeeper's Guide to Budgies*, Tetra Press, 1988.

Alderton, David, *You and Your Pet Bird*, Alfred A. Knopf, 1994.

Doane, Bonnie Munro, *Parrot Training: A Guide to Taming and Gentling Your Avian Companion,* Howell Book House, 2001.

Forshaw, Joseph, *Atlas of Parrots of the World,* Illustrations by William Cooper, TFH Publications, 1991.

Gallerstein, Gary A., DVM, *The Complete Bird Owner's Handbook*, Avian Publications, 2003.

Grindol, Diane, and Tom Roudybush, *Teaching Your Bird to Talk*, Howell Book House, 2003.

Hubbard, Jennifer, *The New Parrot Training Handbook: A Complete Guide to Taming and Training Your Pet Bird*, Parrot Press, 1997.

McCluggage, David, DVM, and Pamela L. Higdon, *Holistic Care for Birds*, Howell Book House, 1999.

O'Neil, Jacqueline, *The Complete Idiot's Guide to Bird Care & Training*, Alpha Books, 1998.

Rach, Julie, *Why Does My Bird Do That?,* Howell Book House, 1998.

Magazines

Bird Talk
Monthly magazine devoted to pet bird ownership. Subscription information:
P.O. Box 57347
Boulder, CO 80322-7347
www.birdtalkmagazine.com

Birds USA
Annual magazine aimed at first-time bird owners. Look for it in your local bookstore or pet store.
www.birdtalkmagazine.com

Bird Times
This magazine for pet bird owners is published six times a year. Subscription information:
Pet Publishing, Inc.
7-L Dundas Circle
Greensboro, NC 27407
www.petpublishing.com/birdtimes

Online Resources

Bird-specific sites have been cropping up regularly on the Internet. These sites offer pet bird owners the opportunity to share stories about their pets and trade helpful hints about bird care.

To find an avian veterinarian, visit the **Association of Avian Veterinarians** at www.aav.org. To find a holistic avian veterinarian in your area, visit the **American Holistic Veterinary Medical Association** at www.ahvma.org. Both sites offer ways to search for practitioners in your area.

Bird Clubs

The American Budgerigar Society
863 Highland Ave. NW
Palm Bay, FL 32907
www.abs1.org

The American Federation of Aviculture
P.O. Box 7312
N. Kansas City, MO 64116
www.afabirds.org

Avicultural Society of America
P.O. Box 5516
Riverside, CA 92517-5517

Avicultural Society of Australia
49 Harold St.
Buleen, 3106
Australia
www.birds.org.au

The Budgerigar Society
Spring Gardens
Northampton
NN1 1DR
Britain
www.budgerigarsociety.com

International Aviculturists Society
P.O. Box 341852
Memphis, TN 38184
www.funnyfarmexotics.com/IAS/

Society of Parrot Breeders and Exhibitors
P.O. Box 546
Hollis, NH 03049
www.spbe.org

Pet Loss Resources

ASPCA National Pet Loss Hotline
(212) 876-7700, ext. 4355

Chicago Veterinary Medical Association Pet Loss Support Helpline
(630) 325-1600

Pet Grief Support Service
(602) 995-5885

Pet Loss.net
www.pet-loss.net

University of California, Davis
www.vetmed.ucdavis.edu/petloss/index.htm

Colorado State University
www.argusinstitute.colostate.edu/grief.htm

Cornell University
web.vet.cornell.edu/public/petloss/

University of Florida
www.vetmed.ufl.edu/vmth/companions.htm

University of Illinois
www.cvm.uiuc.edu/CARE/

Iowa State University
www.vetmed.iastate.edu/animals/petloss/

Michigan State University
cvm.msu.edu/petloss/index.htm

Purdue University
www.vet.purdue.edu/chab/bond.htm

University of Tennessee
www.vet.utk.edu/hero/animalserv/petloss.htm

Tufts University
www.tufts.edu/vet/petloss/

Washington State University
www.vetmed.wsu.edu/plhl/index.htm

Index

abnormal behaviors, illness, 106
acquisition sources, 22–24
acrylic cages, purchasing guidelines, 32
adult birds, age determination, 22–23
aerobics, bird behaviors, 101
ages, determination factors, 22–23
aggression, territorial, 26
Alexander the Great, 17
Alexandrine parakeet, 17
Amazon parrot, life spans, 14
anatomy
    cardiovascular system, 71
    digestive system, 71–73
    elements illustrated, 10
    English versus American parakeets,
      20–21
    feathers, 73–74
    nervous system, 73
    physical traits, 14
    respiratory system, 70–71
    skeletal system, 69–70
    skin, 69
animal bites, first aid treatment, 87
apartments, ownership, 12–13
articular gout, symptoms/treatment, 84
Association of Avian Veterinarians, 52–53
audiotapes, escaped bird recapture, 67
Australia, development, 12, 13, 19
avian flu, cautions/concerns, 94
avian veterinarians. See veterinarians

background noise, cage location, 37
bamboo cages, purchasing, 33
bathing, guidelines, 61

BBC's Cage Word Contest, parakeet
  vocabulary record, 115
beaks, 14, 23, 53, 87, 100, 101
behaviors
    abnormal, 106
    aerobics, 101
    beak grinding, 100
    beak wiping, 101
    eye pining, 101
    feather picking, 101–102, 103
    fluffing, 102, 103
    jealousy, 102
    mutual preening, 102–103
    one-foot-resting, 104
    pair bonding, 103
    physical punishment, 111–112
    preening, 103
    regurgitating, 104
    scratching, 104
    side-stepping, 104
    stress indicators, 105–106
    territorial aggression, 26
    vocalizations, 104–105
Belgium, parakeet development, 20
birdkeeping, 12–13, 17–20
bird marts, parakeet source, 23
bird shows, parakeet source, 23
birds (other), introduction, 26–27
bleeding, first aid treatment, 88
blood feathers, first aid, 65
blow dryers, bathing element, 61
boarding services, travel, 50, 51
boldness, parakeet selection element, 24
bonding, ownership reason, 14

breeders, parakeet source, 23
budgerigar, alternative name, 13
budgie, alternative name, 13
bumblefoot, symptoms/treatment, 85
burns, first aid treatment, 89

cages
    acrylic versus wire, 32–33
    bamboo, 33
    cleaning guidelines, 48
    cover application timeline, 46
    covers, 35, 36
    door considerations, 34
    dropping observation, 72
    escaped bird recapture, 67
    gravel paper (sandpaper), 34–35
    location guidelines, 36, 37
    new toy introduction, 41
    playgym location, 42
    purchasing guidelines, 30–35
    setup guidelines, 36
    size guidelines, 31
    tray considerations, 34–35
    wooden, 33
canaries, Dutch development history, 18
cardiovascular system, 71
Centers for Disease Control and
    Prevention, avian flu, 94
ceres, male versus female, 25
chemicals, parrot-proofing, 43–44
children, 15–16, 96–97
classified ads, parakeet source, 22–23
cleaning, cages, 47
cleaning products, parrot-proofing, 43
cloacal prolapse, first aid treatment, 90
close-link chains, safety issues, 40, 41
cockatoos, life spans, 14
coin drop, trick training, 116
colors, 12, 13, 25, 74
companionship, ownership reason, 14
concrete grooming perches, 39
concussions, first aid treatment, 89
covers, 35, 36, 46

crosswalk trick, trick training, 116–117
curiosity, 24, 42–43

death recovery, guidelines, 96–97
digestive system, anatomy, 71–73
dishes, food/water, 38
doors, cage considerations, 34
droppings, 47, 48, 72, 94

eagle pose, trick training, 118–119
ears, hearing sense, 75
egg binding, first aid treatment, 90
Egypt, birdkeeping history, 17
emergency care, guidelines, 89
Europe, development, 12, 18–20
eyes, 22–23, 75, 90, 95, 101

face masks, age determination factors, 22
faces, scaly face, 82–83
feathers, 22–23, 62–65, 73–74, 86,
    101–103
fecal material, 47, 48, 72, 94
feeders, covered versus uncovered, 38
feet, 34–35, 39, 40, 76, 85, 89, 104
females, ownership reasons, 25
first aid, 89–96
fliers, escaped bird recapture, 68
flooring, cage tray considerations, 34–35
food dishes, purchasing guidelines, 38
foods, 52–59, 80, 84–85, 104
foreign objects, first aid treatment, 91
fractures, first aid treatment, 90
France, parakeet development history, 20
French moult, symptoms/treatment, 86
friends, travel alternative, 50, 51
frostbite, first aid treatment, 90
fruits, dietary guidelines, 54–55

giardia, symptoms/treatment, 86
goiter, symptoms/treatment, 83–84
goldfinches, birdkeeping history, 18
gout, symptoms/treatment, 84
grains, dietary guidelines, 53

gravel paper (sandpaper), 34–35, 40
Greece, birdkeeping history, 17
grit, dietary guidelines, 58
grooming, 61–66
Guinness Book of Records, 14, 115

handling, 16, 107–111
head nodding, trick training, 118
heads, 14, 22, 104
health
    abnormal behavior, 106
    dropping observation, 72
    first aid situations/treatment, 87–93
    good health indicators, 25
    holiday precautions, 50
    homeopathic treatments, 81
    human food cautions/concerns, 56
    illness indicators, 47, 78
    injected medications, 81–82
    oral medications, 80
    stress indicators, 105–106
    temperature fluctuation, 49
    topical medications, 82
health problems, 82–87, 94–97
hearing, sense component, 76
holidays, 16, 50
Holland, Dutch canaries, 18
homemade toys, guidelines, 41
homeopathic treatments, 81
homing abilities, 16
human foods, dietary guidelines, 55–56

injected medications, 81–82
interaction, ownership advantage, 13

jealousy, problem behavior, 102
jingle-type bells, safety issues, 41

kidneys, gout concerns, 84
knemidokoptes mites, scaly face, 82–83

larks, birdkeeping history 18
lead poisoning, first aid treatment, 91–92

lead-weighted toys, safety, 41
leather thongs, safety, 40
leftovers, dietary guidelines, 55–56
legs, 84, 90
legumes, dietary guidelines, 53
life spans, 13–14
lifestyles, ownership, 12–15
lipoma, symptoms/treatment, 85
lost birds, escapes, 66–68

males, ownership reasons, 25
manzanita branches, perch material, 39
mealtimes, bathing opportunity, 61
medications, 81–82
minerals, dietary guidelines, 58
mirrors, socialization issues, 41
mite protectors, cautions/concerns, 68
mites, knemidokoptes, 82–83
molting, natural grooming, 63, 66
monk (Quaker) parakeets, 50
mouths, 76
multiple birds, 25–27, 102–103

nails, 41, 62
National Association of Professional Pet
    Sitters, 51
necks, 14, 22
nervous system, anatomy element, 73
noise (radio/TV), cage location, 37
nonstick cookware, 44–45

obesity, symptoms/treatment, 84–85
older birds, health concerns, 95
one-foot-resting, normal behavior, 104
oral medications, 80
organic produce, dietary guidelines, 55
overheating, first aid treatment, 92

papillomas, symptoms/treatment, 86
parrot-proofing, guidelines, 43–45
parrots, life spans, 14
PBFDS (psittacine beak and feather dis-
    ease syndrome), 86–87

pellets, dietary guidelines, 56–57
perches, 36, 38–40, 48
pet sitters, travel alternative, 50, 51
pets (other), parrot-proofing element, 44
pet stores, parakeet source, 23–24
petting, taming technique, 110–111
physical punishment, avoiding, 111–112
plants, safety/health issues, 45
plastic toys, safety issues, 41
playgyms, 42, 48
playing dead, trick training, 119
playtime, household hazards, 42–43
poisoning, first aid treatment, 93
popularity, reasons for, 21
posing (like an eagle), trick, 118–119
preening, natural grooming, 60
proteins, dietary guidelines, 55
psittacine beak and feather disease
    syndrome (PBFDS), 86–87
PVC tubes, perch material, 39

Quaker (monk) parakeets, 50
quarantine, 27, 50
questions, veterinarian selection, 78–79

radio/TV, cage location guidelines, 37
regurgitation, normal behavior, 104
relatives, travel alternative, 50, 51
renters, ownership advantages, 12–13
resources, 120–122
respiratory system, 70–71, 88–89
ring toys, safety issues, 41
Rome, birdkeeping history, 17–18
ropes, perch material, 39
rope toys, safety issues, 40–41
runts, avoiding, 24

safety, 40–45, 65–68, 87–93
sandpaper (gravel paper), 34–35, 40
scaly face, symptoms/treatment, 82–83
scratching, normal behavior, 104
seasons, 49, 63, 66

seed-only diets, goiter concerns, 83–84
seeds, 53, 54
seizures, first aid treatment, 93
self-cleaning ovens, parrot-proofing, 45
senses, 75–76
shell parrot, alternative name, 13
shock, first aid treatment, 93
shyness, parakeet selection element, 24
side-stepping, normal behavior, 104
sight, sense component, 76
skeletal system, anatomy element, 69–70
skin, 69, 86
sleepiness, parakeet selection, 24
smell, sense component, 76
socialization, mirror concerns, 41
step up/step down, taming, 109–110
stress, behavior indicators, 105–106
stripes, age determination factors, 22
supplements, dietary guidelines, 58

talking, 26, 112–116. See also vocaliza-
    tions
taming, techniques, 107–111
taste, sense component, 76
temperature fluctuation, 37, 49, 61, 92
territorial aggression, 26
throat, goiter concerns, 83–84
thyroid gland, 83–84, 95
toes, common traits, 14
toilet training, techniques, 111
topical medications, 82
touch, sense component, 76
toys, 36, 40–41, 48
training, 111–119
travel, guidelines, 49–51
trays, cage considerations, 34–35
tricks, training techniques, 116–119
tumors, older bird concerns, 95
TV/radio, cage location guidelines, 37

United States, parakeet history, 20

vegetables, dietary guidelines, 54–55
veterinarians, 50, 51, 68, 77, 79–82
visceral gout, symptoms/treatment, 84
vision problems, older bird concerns, 95
vitamins, dietary guidelines, 53–54, 58
vocalizations. *See also* talking
    reasons for, 104–105
    talk training techniques, 112–116

warbling grass parakeet, 13
water, 38, 59, 80

water dishes, purchasing, 38
weather, 49, 61
wings, 62–68
wire cages, purchase guidelines, 33
wooden cages, purchasing, 33
wooden toys, safety issues, 40

young birds, 22–23, 25

zebra parrot, alternative name, 13
zoonotic diseases, cautions/concerns, 94